BOSTON BRONZE & STONE SPEAK TO US

Other books by Joseph R. Gallo, Jr.

101 Plantcare Tips for Your Interior Plantscape

BOSTON

Bronze & Stone Speak To Us

JOSEPH R. GALLO, JR.

HANOVER STREET PRESS
Boston, Massachusetts

ISBN: 978-1-61364-631-1

Published by Hanover Street Press

All photography by Joseph R. Gallo, Jr.

To order additional copies email joe@pdiplants.com

Maps, cover design, book design and layout by Kathleen Valentine, Valentine-Design.com of Gloucester

Printed in China

About the Maps

The maps shown at the beginning of each chapter are included to give an indication of the placement of the featured works. They are not comprehensive. If you are unfamiliar with Boston streets, please consult a detailed map of city streets for more complete directions. The number within the the red star corresponds with the page number describing the monument. The red stars approximately indicate the geographical location of the monuments.

I dedicate this book to my wife Jeannine,
my daughter Carolyne, and my son Greg.

This book is also dedicated to Mayor Thomas M. Menino,
guardian of the city of Boston's people and their
monuments' pristine up-keep during these past twenty years
and to the Citizens of the City of Boston

Symbols mean nothing if the values aren't there. We didn't spend millions of dollars just so that the Statue wouldn't fall into the harbor and become a hazard to navigation. We didn't fix up Ellis Island so that people would have a nice place to go on a Sunday afternoon. We did it because we wanted to restore, remember, and renew the basic values that made America great.
- Lee Iacocca, The Chairman of the Save the Statue of Liberty Foundation

"Memor et Fidelis"
MINDFUL AND FAITHFUL

"Boston is your Mistress," my wife sometimes says because of the numerous times I sneak out of our waterfront condo in The North End to take photos of the statues and monuments ornamenting the streets and parks of Boston or in copying their stone carved inscriptions. The hours spent in my study absorbed in my computer typing this little guidebook for our city's visitors involved much time spent away from my loving wife, Jeannine.

Thank you for your understanding and patience.

Compiling updated photos and historical text for the creation of a much needed, simple to use, guide book for educating our Boston visitors from all over the world about our City of Boston's Bronze and Stone Monuments was time consuming, but fulfilling. The purpose and meaning of these monuments is, I hope, made more lucid by this new book.

TABLE OF CONTENTS

BOSTON
AN IMMIGRANT'S GATEWAY

America's promise has drawn people from all corners of the world to Boston, in search of a better life for themselves and their families. Their traditions and values have become the fabric of our neighborhoods.

Here in Boston we seek to fulfill that promise by providing a life filled with peace, dignity and opportunity for all who make this great city their home.

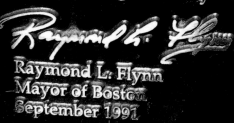

Raymond L. Flynn
Mayor of Boston
September 1991

What is Public Art

Public art fills a much broader definition than art in a gallery or a museum. In simple terms, public art is any work of art or design that is created by an artist specifically to be sited in a public space. It can tower several stories high, or it can call attention to the pavement beneath your feet. It can be cast, carved, built, assembled, or painted. Whatever its form, public art attracts attention. By its presence alone, public art can heighten our awareness, question our assumptions, transform a landscape, or express community values, and for these reasons it can have the power, over time, to transform a city's image. Public art helps define an entire community's identity and reveal the unique character of a specific neighborhood. It is a unifying force.

Why Public Art?

The impact of public art on a community is priceless and immeasurable and once experienced it only appreciates. Public art has the power to energize our public spaces, arouse our thinking, and transform the places where we live, work, and play into more welcoming and beautiful environments that invite interaction. Public art can make strangers talk, children ask questions, and calm a hurried life. It enhances the quality of life by encouraging a heightened sense of place and by introducing people to works of art that can touch them and the generations to come.

The Many Benefits of Public Art

Beyond its enriching personal benefits, public art is a true symbol of a city's maturity. It increases a community's assets and expresses a community's positive sense of identity and values. It helps green space thrive, enhances roadsides, pedestrian corridors, and community gateways; it demonstrates unquestionable civic and corporate pride in citizenship and affirms an educational environment. A city with public art is a city that thinks and feels. (nnpaf.org/what_is_art.html - Nov. 26, 2010).

The City of Boston has become a rich environment for Public Art.

The Meaning of "Statue"

A statue is a sculpture in the round, representing a person or persons -- normally full-length, as opposed to a bust and at least close to life-size or larger -- an animal, or an event. Its primary form is representational. The definition of a statue is not always clear-cut; sculptures of a person on a horse, called equestrian statues, are certainly included, and in many cases, such as a Madonna and Child or a Pietá, a sculpture can be of two people. A small statue, usually small enough to be picked up, is called a statuette or figurine.

Many statues are built on commission to commemorate a historical event, or the life of an influential person. Many statues are intended as public art, exhibited outdoors, or in public buildings for the edification of passers-by, with a larger impact than ordinary words could ever have for the common man.

INTRODUCTION

———————◆———————

Sculpture is the physical embodiment of an artist's spiritual perception of an individual, an event or a dream, cast in bronze or sculpted from stone for all of us to admire and wonder about. The artist/sculptor captures the spirit of a human experience; be it an accomplishment, an invention, an idea, a creation, whether it be mystical, historical, educational, political, military, heroic, literary, poetic, artistic, mechanical, or adventurous, it must speak to us, the viewer, through the medium of bronze or stone. The selection and arrangement of these bronzes and stones were, of course, matters of considerable discussion.

Some selections are so obvious that failure to include them would arouse the collective wrath of those already well acquainted with the history of the City of Boston. Actually, the choice of what monument is included and what is not included in such a guidebook will probably create much more controversy than the way in which they are arranged. The selection of some of these figures will perhaps baffle some readers; the omission of other figures will certainly upset others. However, that kind of dissent is inevitable in any project based on personal decisions and subjective judgments. I will leave it to my readers to reflect upon the long and fascinating history of Boston, and decide for themselves which monuments to men, women, or events would be their choice to be selected and discussed here.

All the bronzes and stones depicted in this book reflect the artists' attempts to capture the Spirit of the person or event to be celebrated by the people of Boston, who funded and erected these statues as symbolic milestones, marking both the people and accomplishments throughout our city's almost 400 year history.

To reside in this livable, walkable city is so much different then just visiting it. To visit Boston is still a delight. This book has kept me away periodically from my wife of twenty-three years because of all the Muses calling me to write about and photograph my historical city -- this city that I have always loved. These bronze and stone monumental sentinels of Boston embody the individuals, the events of the past, and the future aspirations of, not only Boston's, but America's future generations.

This sometimes eclectic selection of unusual and often contradictory monuments seems to me somewhat symbolic of the idiosyncratic character of Boston itself. I have always thought that one of the more lovable and distinctive aspects of Boston is the rather haphazard way in which its buildings cluster together, a time capsule stuffed with colonial meetinghouses, Federal townhouses, and Greek Revival market buildings side by side with Victorian mansions, Gothic Revival cathedrals, and high-rise skyscrapers. They are all separate and distinctive, just like our great city's monuments, and yet they all merge into a striking unity that conveys something of the distinctiveness of the City of Boston.

"Abraham Lincoln used to say that the test of one's Americanism was not one's family tree; the test was how much one believed in America. Because we're like a religion, really. A secular religion. We believe in ideas and ideals. We're not one race, we're many; we're not one ethnic group, we're everyone; we don't speak only one language, we're all of these people. We're tied together by our belief in political democracy, in religious freedom, in capitalism, a free economy where people make their own choices about the spending of their money. We're tied together because we respect human life, and because we respect the rule of law." (Giuliani, p. xvi)

Boston is all of the above. Boston is America, America is Boston.

A CALLING

Every morning, at 8:00 am, I wake up to the sound of a cannon from the USS Constitution and hear it again at sunset. The church bells of Old North Church, Saint Stephen's, and Saint Leonard's ring, all calling me, summoning me to tell the stories of Boston's heroes, heroines and momentous memorable events of the distant past as well as its most recent era. A student of American History, an appreciator of sculpture, my purpose in this book is to simply further educate myself and others about the greatness of the City of Boston, by better understanding the bronze and stone statues and monuments that surround us.

ACKNOWLEDGEMENTS

———————◆———————

I would like to thank my daughter Carolyne A. Gallo for all her patience and effective editing of this work in the beginning stages of this book, her untiring hours on the laptop, compiling the words and images that make this book so unique, and the organizing of all the geographical locations of these monuments making it easily accessible for the layman to find and learn about these historical sentinels of Boston.

I also want to thank Pamela Veerman for her long hours typing and final editing of this book.

Special thanks to Kathleen Valentine for all her guidance and direction in building this book. An author herself, she encouraged me to go forward with not only an informative book but a book of beauty, creating the front and back covers and assisting me in the final design of this guidebook itself.

In addition, I would like to thank Dr. Louis E. Jordan III for setting me in the right direction academically with the historical aspects of this book and for his studious Latin translations of some of the monument's inscriptions and accompanying me on much of the photography of these monuments, while meandering through the streets of Boston.

Thank you to Sarah Hutt, former Director of the Boston Art Commission, City of Boston, for her kind direction, encouragement and giving of statue and monument information in her departments possession that made this book possible. Thank you to Susan Greendyke from the Boston State House, to art curator and consultant Rebecca Reynolds.

To Kathy and Bob Shure, thank you for your contributions of photos and text from your archives at Skylight Studios on the following works of art: *In Tribute to Boston Police Officers, The Wentworth Leopard, Cy Young, Police and Fireman Memorial and Hear Us - State House Women's Leadership Project.*

Thank you also to Mayor Thomas M. Menino, Toni Pollak and the Boston Park Department for preserving Boston's past by maintaining Boston's bronze and stone monuments throughout our City of Boston enabling me to take such beautiful photographs for this guidebook.

Special thanks again to my wife Jeannine for her patience and contribution with my writing and researching this little guide book. The hours in these past five years has been very demanding for both of us.

PREFACE

The purpose for writing this book is threefold. First, the growing inventory of monuments dedicated to individuals, events and themes within and around the city of Boston since 1993 needed updating. Second, because of these new works and an absence of any official map of these statues, I feel this easy-to-use guidebook with handy maps is necessary. Third, by grouping these monuments according to their geographical locations, Boston natives and the millions who visit here each year, can tour our city more efficiently, more knowledgeably and more enjoyably. As a Bostonian myself I wanted to celebrate these monuments of bronze and stone and remind us of the incredible history this great city of Boston possesses for the every day visitor. These bronze and stone monuments celebrate almost 400 years of Boston history.

This book appreciates the creative works of the sculptors, and of the historians, who supplied the foundation of this guidebook.

Born and raised within and around Boston, I discovered the history and culture through family and school visits into the city. Even as a boy, I noticed the quiet murmurs of these solid bronze and stone monuments whispering to me. As I matured, obtaining my education in the city at the University of Massachusetts at Boston, these monuments began speaking their messages louder from their inscriptions proclaiming innovative financial institutions, new educational systems, diverse religions, creative arts, immigrant cultures, sociology, philanthropies, athletic heroes, medical accomplishments, literary achievements, military feats, humorous whimsical themes, and ethnic leaderships. These monuments speak to all of us and are engraved in metal and granite to inspire generations of future Bostonians, all Americans and her visitors.

This book heavily relies on the past works of Allen Forbes' "Some Statues of Boston" and "Other Statues of Boston", both out of print (1946), as well as Dr. Walter Muir Whitehill's "Statues of Boston" (1976). In addition, much reference is taken from Marty Carlocks' monumental work entitled "A Guide to Public Art in Greater Boston" (1993).

Since the 1600s to the present day, much has been accomplished in the City of Boston. These silent teachers in bronze and stone tell this city's story well, we just have to read their inscriptions and listen to their whispers.

Joseph R. Gallo Jr.

A Bostonian

Boston Common
BRONZES & STONES

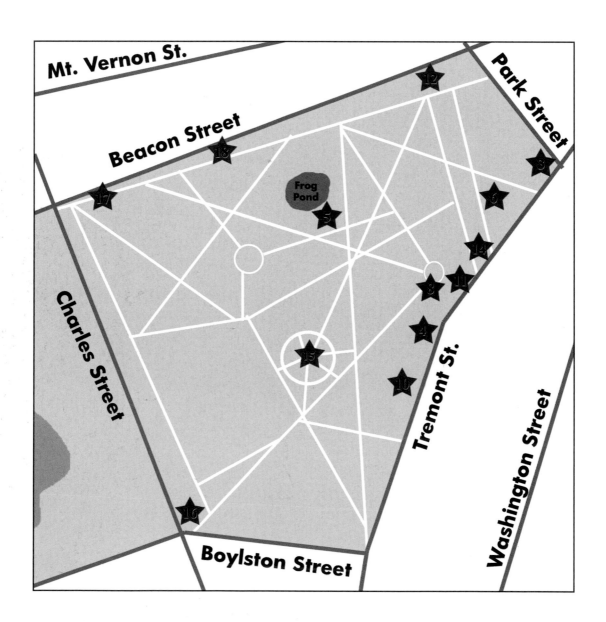

BOSTON COMMON TABLET 1913

Boston Common/ Park Street
R. Clipston Sturgis (1860-1955), Sculptor / designer
Slate Tablet set in Granite

This tablet was erected in 1913 to commemorate the sale of the property we now know as the Boston Common. It was sold by William Blaxton (Blackstone) to the Town of Boston in 1634.

The artist is R. Clipston Sturgis.

BOSTON MASSACRE MONUMENT 1888

Boston Common /Lafayette Mall Tremont Street
Robert Kraus (1850-1902), Sculptor
Bronze / Stone

Freedom is symbolically victorious, cast in this bronze sculpture by Kraus.

This very dramatic Freedom, depicted with the flag, a broken chain, an American eagle, and a trod-upon British crown, are positioned before a column with the names of the five Bostonians killed by British soldiers in the 1770 encounter. The high relief bronze plaque depicting the massacre features an extended hand which visitors love to shake, keeping it polished. Crispus Attucks, famed as the first black to give his life for this nation, lies in the foreground. His shoe also protrudes from the relief and visitors keep that polished as well.

FISHING IN THE FROG POND

2003, Boston Common / Lafayette Mall
David Phillips, Sculptor
Bronze

This kid-friendly sculpture has always been a delight for me and every other kid who has visited Boston Commons' Frog Pond. Two 4-foot-high bronze frog sculptures watch over the winter skaters and summer waders at the Frog Pond on Boston Common. From their perch on the eastern end of the pond, they look across Charles Street to the trees in the Boston Public Garden. According to Joseph Bagley, if you were standing on the same spot 8,000 years earlier, the pond would still be there inhabited by real, not bronze, frogs. In place of the skaters and waders, you'd find indigenous peoples living around the pond, and thousands of clamshells would be visible, scattered along a shoreline reaching as far as Charles Street. Bagley, a recent archaeology graduate, easily paints this picture—the fruit of senior work for distinction, funded by UROP, in which he studied artifacts excavated from the area around the Frog Pond.

www.phillipssculpture.com/resume.htm (21 Oct. 2010)

THE BREWER FOUNTAIN
CONTAINING POSEIDON, AMPHITRITE, GALATEA AND ACIS (1855)

Boston Public Gardens Tremont / Temple Streets
Jean Auguste Edouard Liénard, French Sculptor
Bronze

One of the most conspicuous objects on Boston Common, standing near the wall at Park and Tremont Streets, is the Brewer Fountain. The fountain was a gift to the city by Gardner Brewer, which began to function for the first time on June 3, 1868. It is a copy, in bronze, of a fountain designed by French artist (Jean Auguste Edouard Liénard, most likely). The fountain was sculpted for the Paris Word's Fair of 1855 Exposition Universelle de 1855, where it was awarded a gold medal.

The great figures at the base represent Neptune (Roman god of water and sea), Amphitrite (Greek sea goddess), Acis [spirit of Acis River by Roman Poet Ovid], and Galatea (Roman sea nymph). The fountain was cast in Paris, brought to this country, and set up at the sole expense of the public-spirited donor. Copies of iron were made for the cities of Lyons and Bordeaux; and an exact copy in bronze was made for Said Pacha, a late Viceroy of Egypt.

Gardner Brewer was born in Boston in 1800 and died in Newport, RI in 1874. He was one of the wealthiest and most liberal of Boston merchants. After attaining his maturity he was for some time a distiller, but afterward engaged in the dry-goods trade, and founded the house of Gardner Brewer & Co., which represented some of the largest mills in New England, and had branches in New York and Philadelphia.

In the dry-goods business, by accurate method combined with great sagacity, he accumulated a fortune which, at his death, was estimated at several million dollars.

Mr. Brewer at one time took an active part in politics as a Republican. He was also a strong protectionist, and took great interest in the industrial development of the country. He used his large wealth liberally for the public good, and shortly before his death gave to the city of Boston this beautiful fountain, which stands at an angle on Boston Common. (http://www.celebrateboston.com/sites/boston-common-brewer-fountain.htm Dec. 14, 2010).

PARKMAN PLAZA
LEARNING, INDUSTRY, & RELIGION 1958-60

Boston Common / Tremont Street
Arcangelo Cascieri (1902-1997) and Adio di Biccari (1914 -2009), Sculptors
Bronze / Granite

Dedicated to the Memory of George E. Parkman (1823-1908)
Through whose Beneficence Lafayette Mall was Improved and this Plaza created (1958-1960)
- Honorable John R. Collins and Honorable John B. Hines -- Mayors of Boston

Crowds surround the courthouse. The grisly murder trial is the talk of the town. All of Boston is poised, waiting for the verdict, and the media cover every twist and turn of the testimony. Is it the recent "hockey dad" murder trial? No, far from it. The year is 1849, and a Harvard Medical School professor is on trial for the murder of George Parkman, the wealthy Boston Brahmin who donated the land for the school's campus just a few years before his grisly death -- and dismemberment.

Professor John Webster is found guilty, and the fiscally poor but socially respectable gentleman swings from the gibbet. The murder and its aftermath are so remarkable that when Charles Dickens visits Boston in 1867, one of his first requests is to see the room where Parkman was murdered. "Ah," said Dickens. "You sick bastard."

Once known as the victim of America's "most celebrated murder," Parkman left behind a legacy of public service, a sizable estate and two children -- including the imaginatively named George F. Parkman.

Fast-forward to 1908. Parkman Jr. dies of unsensational causes, leaving Boston five million dollars for the improvement of parks. Four years later, the Parkman Bandstand is built and dedicated to him on the Boston Common, at the extravagant cost of $1 million.

Fast-forward again to 1960, when Boston Mayor John F. Collins dedicates the completed Parkman Plaza to George F. Parkman (the younger). It is a little semicircular patch of pavement on the Common, bracketed by three inspirational statues celebrating the virtues of Learning, Industry and Religion.

(http://www.flakmag.com/misc/parkman.html Jan 30, 2011)

DECLARATION OF INDEPENDENCE MONUMENT

Tremont Street / Boston Common
John Paramino, Sculptor
Bronze Plaque / Stone

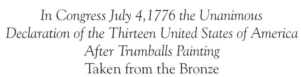

In Congress July 4, 1776 the Unanimous
Declaration of the Thirteen United States of America
After Trumballs Painting
Taken from the Bronze

The United States Declaration of Independence is a statement adopted by the Continental Congress on July 4, 1776, which announced that the thirteen American colonies, then at war with Great Britain, were now independent states, and thus no longer a part of the British Empire. Written primarily by Thomas Jefferson, the Declaration is a formal explanation of why Congress had voted on July 2 to declare independence from Great Britain, more than a year after the outbreak of the American Revolutionary War. The birthday of the United States of America, Independence Day -- is celebrated on July 4, the day the wording of the Declaration was approved by Congress.

The Declaration justified the independence of the United States by listing colonial grievances against King George III, and by asserting certain natural rights, including a right of revolution. Having served its original purpose in announcing independence, the text of the Declaration was initially ignored after the American Revolution. Its stature grew over the years, particularly the second sentence, a sweeping statement of individual human rights:

"We hold these truths to be self-evident, that all men are created equal, that they are endowed by their Creator with certain unalienable Rights, that among these are Life, Liberty and the Pursuit of Happiness." This sentence has been called "one of the best-known sentences in the English language" and "the most potent and consequential words in American history."

LAFAYETTE MALL MONUMENT

Boston Common / Lafayette Mall
John F. Paramino, Sculptor
Bronze Plaque / Stone

I am so proud to think that in 1824 General Lafayette walked this very street, Tremont Street, that I walk today. I am impressed that this French General took part in laying the corner stone of Bunker Hill and entering The Old North Church to view America's first marble sculpture of his friend and military ally, George Washington.

This Mall named in honor of Marquis De Lafayette
Distinguished French Solider
Mayor-General in the War of American Independence and Illustrious Patriot of the French Revolution who Nobly served the cause of the Liberty on the Continents
Invited by Act of Congress to Revisit the United States as Guest of the Nation in 1824
He was Welcomed with Signal Honor as He Passed Along this Mall
He laid the Corner stone of the Bunker Hill Monument June 17, 1825
'Heaven Saw Fit to Ordain that the Electric Spark of Liberty Should be Conducted Through You From the New World to the Old'.
Erected by the City of Boston 1924.
Taken from the Bronze

ROBERT GOULD SHAW
AND THE 54TH MASSACHUSETTS REGIMENT BOSTON COMMON / PARK ST.

Augustus Saint-Gaudens (1848 - 1907), Sculptor
Bronze Bas-Relief

Born in Ireland, the son of a cobbler, Saint-Gaudens was raised in New York where he began as a cameo-cutter. After studying in Paris and Rome, Saint-Gaudens worked in New York and Cornish, NH. His design synthesized vigorous naturalism with abstract ideals. The allegorical sculpture for The Adams Memorial in Washington, D.C.'s Rock Creek Cemetery is his best known work.

The finest of all the individual Boston memorials to participants in the Civil War is the great bronze bas-relief by Augustus Saint-Gaudens (1848-1907) that commemorates the twenty-six-year-old Colonel Robert Gould Shaw and the free Negroes of the 54th Massachusetts Regiment who fell with him on 18 July 1863 in the assault of Fort Wagner, South Carolina. The monument stands on the South side of Beacon Street, facing the State House, past which this first black regiment marched on 28 May 1863 to salute Governor John A. Andrew as it was about to embark for South Carolina. Although Governor Andrew called a meeting in the fall of 1865 to procure an equestrian statue of Shaw by William Wetmore Story, the effort dragged. In 1884 when Saint-Gaudens was given the commission be proposed a bas-relief, but was so incredibly slow in its completion that the monument was only dedicated on 31 May 1897. It was fine enough to have been worth waiting for. (Whitehill, 50)

The memorial occupies one of the most conspicuous places in Boston, opposite the State House, and has been much admired. The sculptor was Saint-Gaudens, the architects sharing the responsibility being H.H. Richardson and Charles McKim. Fourteen years were consumed before the final report of the committee was made by the Treasurer, Edward Atkinson, and during that interval seventeen members of the original committee of twenty-one had died. The memorial committee declared its purpose in these words:

"The monument is intended not only to mark the public gratitude to the fallen hero, who at a critical moment assumed a perilous responsibility, but also to commemorate that great event, wherein he was a leader by which the title of colored men as citizen-soldiers was fixed beyond recall. In such a work all who honor youthful dedication to a noble cause and who rejoice in the triumph of freedom should have an opportunity to contribute."

Part of the inscription written by Charles W. Eliot, who wrote most of the inscriptions during his day, reads: "Together they gave to the nation and the world undying proof that Americans of African descent possess the pride, courage and devotion of the patriot soldier. One hundred and eighty thousand such Americans enlisted under the Union flag."

These words also appear: "O fair haired northern hero with thy guard of dusky hue, up from the field of battle rise to the last review."

The unveiling took place on May 31, 1897, as the flag on the State House was dipped. Governor Wolcott in his address said: "On that day the world learned to know that whatever the color of the skin, the blood that flowed in the veins of the colored man was red with the lusty hue of manhood and of heroism."

Major Higginson made an address in Sanders Theatre, Cambridge, the day before the dedication, and Booker T. Washington made one at Tuskegee. The former said "Negroes had won their places as brave, steady soldiers." Colonial Charles Russell Lowell in his memories of the war wrote: "I can see him now, - Colonel Shaw, - riding with his hat off as he passed the balcony where Mrs. Mary Lowell Putnam stood, to greet her and thus to express the thanks of the Fifty-fourth Regiment for the banner which she had presented."

(Forbes and Eastman, 63)

Commodore John Barry (1949)

Tremont Street / Lafayette Mall
John F. Paramino, Sculptor
Granite

Father of the American Navy
Born in Wexford, Ireland 1745 - Died in Philadelphia 1803
Receive First Commission from the Continental Congress to Command the Lexington
1775
Sailed from Boston on the Raleich 1778
Acclaimed in Boston in 1780 for the Victories on the Alliance
Appointed in 1794 by President Washington to plan Construction of the later to be in
Command of First U.S. Navy Launched 1798
Erected by the city of Boston James M. Curley Mayor 1949
Taken from the Stone

  John Barry (March 25, 1745 – September 13, 1803) was an officer in the Continental Navy during the American Revolutionary War and later in the United States Navy. He is often credited as "The Father of the American Navy". Barry was born in Tacumshane, County Wexford, Ireland and appointed a Captain in the Continental Navy on December 7, 1775.

  Few Americans are well-acquainted with the gallantry and heroic exploits of Philadelphia's Irish-born naval commander, Commodore John Barry. Obscured by his contemporary, naval commander John Paul Jones, Barry remains to this day, an unsung hero of the young American Republic. As most naval historians note, Barry can be classed on a par with Jones for nautical skill and daring, but he exceeds him in the length of service (17 years) to his adopted country and his fidelity to the nurturing of a permanent American Navy. Indeed, Barry deserves the proud epithet, "Father of the American Navy," a title bestowed on him not by current generations of admirers, but by his contemporaries, who were in the best position to judge.

  In the space of 58 years, this son of a poor Irish farmer rose from humble cabin boy to senior commander of the entire United States fleet. Intrepid in battle, he was humane to his men as well as adversaries and prisoners. Barry's war contributions are unparalleled: he was the first to capture a British war vessel on the high seas; he captured two British ships after being severely wounded in a ferocious sea battle; he quelled three mutinies; he fought on land at the Battles of Trenton and Princeton; he captured over 20 ships including an armed British schooner in the lower Delaware; he authored a Signal Book which established a set of signals used for effective communication between ships; and he fought the last naval battle of the American Revolution aboard the frigate Alliance in 1783. (http://www.ushistory.org/people/commodorebarry.htm Nov. 27).

SOLDIERS AND SAILORS, 1877

Boston Common / Lafayette Mall On Flagstaff Hill
Martin Milmore, Sculptor
Bronze / Granite

Soaring and traditionally monumental for a war memorial, Martin Milmore's monument marks the center of historic Boston Common.

Martin Milmore's success with the Roxbury monument led to his doing the Soldiers' and Sailors' Monument atop Flagstaff Hill on Boston Common, begun in 1871 and completed in 1877. Four statues representing Peace, the Sailor, The Muse of History, and the Soldier, stand at the base of a tall column surmounted by a figure of Liberty. Between the projections on which the statues stand are four bronze reliefs depicting the departure of forces for the war, the Battle of Fort Sumter, the work of the Boston Sanitary Commission, and the return from the war. At the foot of the column stand allegorical figures in high relief representing the sections of the country, the North, South, East, and West. The architectural sense of the design is admirable. The presence of this collective monument did not, however, spare Boston a number of individual memorials of the Civil War. (Whitehill, 48)

EDWARD A FILENE

Boston Common / Lafayette Mall / Boylston St.
George Aarons, Sculptor
Bronze / Stone

Social entrepreneurship and conscientious businessman were Edward Filene's most distinguishable characteristics. Another first for Boston was the first company union which included more benefits for its members.

Edward was one of five children of William Filene and Clara Ballin. William Filene was a German Jewish immigrant from Posen, Prussia, who immigrated to the US in 1848. "A peddler, chiefly of women's apparel" he built up a company composed of several small retail shops and in 1881 founded a department store in Boston.

At the age of 5 Edward was injured in a fall that left him with a permanent limp. After attending high school in Lynn, Massachusetts, Edward passed his entrance exams for Harvard University but gave up his educational ambitions to take over the family business in 1890 when his father became seriously ill. Together with his younger brother Abraham Lincoln Filene, he built the Boston firm of William Filene's Sons, later known as Filene's into a great retail success story.

Edward Filene drew inspiration from the scientific management ideas of Frederick Winslow Taylor. While Taylor is best known for the use of scientific methods to increase workplace efficiency, he was also interested in how to improve the quality of work for employees. Filene is credited with refining a number of novel retailing techniques. Filene's Department Store offered complete and honest descriptions of its merchandise and offered to give customers their "money back if not satisfied".

Although Filene's Basement was not the first 'bargain basement' in the United States, the retail design and later the 'automatic mark-downs' generated excitement and proved very profitable. Filene personally supervised construction of the first basement in Boston. An advocate of consumer education, he introduced color matching tools in the clothing departments of his stores.

Filene was also a pioneer in employee relations. He instituted a profit sharing program, a minimum wage for women, a 40 hour work week, health clinics and paid vacations. He also played an important role in encouraging the Filene Cooperative Association: 'perhaps the earliest American company union'. Through this channel he engaged constructively with his employees in collective bargaining and arbitration processes.

He formed a savings and loan association for employees which later became the Filene Employee's Credit Union.

THE FOUNDERS MEMORIAL, 1930

Boston Common / Beacon and Spruce Streets
John F. Paramino, Sculptor
Bronze Bas-relief / Stone

Boston Founded AD 1630 Tablet
Commissioned by the City of Boston to mark its 300th anniversary.
Taken from the Stone

   This bas-relief plaque depicts the primary meeting between Boston's first settler, the reclusive William Blackston (Blaxton) and John Winthrop. Winthrop and his companions found Charlestown unsatisfactory and crossed to "Shawmut", the peninsula we now know as Boston. Among the figures in the group are the clergyman John Wilson, and Ann Pollard, the first white woman known to step onto Boston's soil.

Oneida Football Club

Boston Common / Beacon / Spruce Streets
Plaque designed by I. Howland Jones;
Bas relief by Joseph Coletti, 1925
Stone

Just another first for Boston. Maybe this is another reason why Boston is such a sports town. Football has its historical roots here.

In 1862, the first football club in America was organized at Boston. Three of the original team members attended Mr. Dixwell's Boston Private Latin School located at Boylston Place (opposite Central Burying Ground on Boston Common). Other team members were recruited from Boston Latin and English High Schools, comprising a total squad of 15 people.

The name of the team was the Oneida Club. It is said that the Oneida's goal line was never crossed, and that losing team members were often greatly reprimanded by their parents for returning home severely bruised and with torn clothing.

Sixteen year-old Gerrit Smith Miller has been credited as the "father" or initiator of the club. Walter Camp, considered the Father of American Football, is quoted in the November 7, 1923 Boston Globe as stating the Oneidas were the first football league in America.

First U.S. Aerial Photo

All the football games were played on Boston Common. The older game was much different than the current professional version. The object was to get a rubber ball across the goal line of the opponent's team. The first team to score two goals won. There weren't many rules or a time limit, and the ball could be kicked, thrown, or just handed over to other team members. According to Boston Ways by George F. Weston Jr. (1957), a game between the Oneida Club and Boston Latin School had lasted two hours and forty-seven minutes, without any interruption at all.

At first, the Oneida Club challenged any on-comers, but eventually the meets were recognized locally as an inter-school sport. The club was disbanded in 1865 after four "seasons," presumably when the members graduated from school. Football was in reality not invented by "Gat" Miller in 1862—Native Americans and Europeans had played many different versions of the game—but the Oneida Club has been recognized as the first organized "league" in America.

A granite tablet is located on Boston Common commemorating the Oneida Club. The tablet is just south of the entrance at Beacon and Spruce Streets. The tablet reads "On this field the Oneida Club of Boston, the first organized football club in the United States, played against all comers from 1862 to 1865 - The Oneida goal was never crossed." The names of team members inscribed on the other side of the tablet. The memorial was unveiled at Boston Common on November 21, 1925, with the surviving members of the team present. (http://www.celebrateboston.com/firsts.htm Nov. 27, 2010)

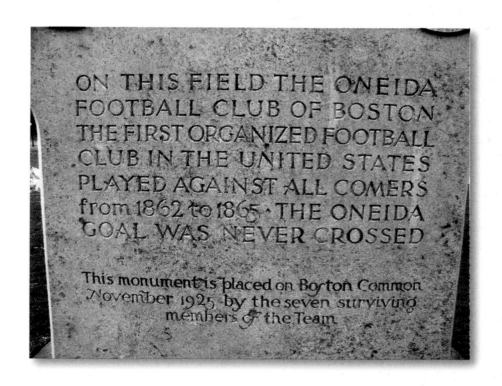

PARTISANS

Boston Common / Charter Street
Sculpture by Andrzes P. Pitynski sited by sculpture placement, Washington D. C.
Bronze

This dynamic inspirational monument is no longer on the Boston Common because of what is documented below, however, this sculpture is an example of how bronze or stone statues can move about our city. For reasons of esthetics, politics or ethics, monuments are sometimes moved. Curiously, these articles below illustrate the dynamic feelings people of our City of Boston have for their Monuments and where they should be placed. Although this article is lengthy, it has a didactic purpose for this book, *Boston Bronze & Stone Speak To Us.*

It has been called everything from a timeless reminder of the 'human toll of fighting for what one believes in' to merely depressing. Now, it is gone.

'Partisans,' the controversial sculpture of five emaciated, be-draggled horsemen that has been at the foot of Boston Common for nearly a quarter-century, has been exiled to storage in South Boston, where it awaits shipment to its owner in San Francisco.

Inspired by the Poles who fought the Nazis and then the communists, 'Partisans' was Polish sculptor Andrew Pitynski's monument to freedom fighters around the world.

But when it came to Boston in 1983, several years after its creation in 1979, it was not always appreciated. The sculpture's international theme, depicted in its tormented horses and gaunt figures, in a park largely devoted to American historical figures, irked some of Boston's art elite. The sculpture was originally loaned to Boston for six months. But its owner, a San Francisco-based foundation, never reclaimed it, according to Sarah Hutt, director of the Boston Art Commission That was an annoyance to parks and police officials, as well as the Beacon Hill community. So the city hired a fine arts moving company to dig up the 8,000-pound sculpture and haul it to a storage facility. 'It's like if you leave your car in front of my house,' said Hutt. 'I can't take it out and wash it. You've got to come and move it.'

Members of the Friends of the Public Garden, which has been asking the city to remove the sculpture for years, voiced strong approval.

'Well, cheers,' said Eugenie Beal, a longtime board member and a Beacon Hill resident. Calling the sculpture's removal during last week's thaw a 'cause for celebration,' Beal said the sculpture had never fit with the rest of the public art on the Common and in the Public Garden, where can be found a figure of George Washington and the Robert Gould Shaw Memorial to the famous 54th Regiment of the Civil War.

'The Boston Common is the first park in the United States, and the monuments on it should have to do with America and its history,' she said. ''Partisans' just isn't appropriate.'

'You do not have to get into an assessment of its artistic value,' she added.

But Pitynski, a 58-year-old Polish immigrant who lives in Brooklyn, NY, and who works in New Jersey, voiced outrage that his monument to freedom fighters had been 'put to the jail.'

'It was my statement from now and for the new generations to come, and they moved the statement out,' he said, adding that no one had told him of its removal.

'I can see some people from the Boston administration maybe hate this statement and hate art,' Pitynski said. When the sculpture first arrived in Boston, it spent a few months on City Hall Plaza, but Mayor Kevin H. White reportedly ordered it moved to the Boston Common, near the corner of Beacon and Charles Streets, where it stayed put. The Boston Art Commission has been trying to get rid of it for much of its time on the Common, Hutt said. The Parks Department also got sick of working around it. That area of the Common has also become a staging area for large events, such as road races and festivals, and police had to deal with people climbing on it during events. It has no solid base, so it had begun sinking, and parts of it could have injured people. Hut said the city has long made it clear to the owner, which she identified as the Sculpture Foundation of San Francisco, that 'Partisans' has overstayed its welcome. Hutt said she did not know why the foundation did not take the sculpture back.'" (The Boston Globe, Wangsness, A1, A14, 1/18/2006)

In August, 1982, Mayor Kevin White received a letter from an unknown art curator outlining plans for bringing to Boston 'a contemporary aesthetic masterpiece,' in the form of a massive aluminum sculpture of Polish patriots on horseback.

'Help,' the mayor's deputy scrawled in a panicked note. 'What is this?!' Confusion and consternation at City Hall have beset Andrew Pitynski's 'Partisans' almost from the moment Boston officials learned of its existence. The debate over where or, indeed, whether the sculpture belonged in Boston is a tortured saga that spanned three mayoral administrations, a 3-inch thick file of official letters, memos, and documents reveals. The drama pitted politicians who feared offending Polish supporters in South Boston against Beacon Hill activists and city arts officials who fretted that the sculpture was out of place and would bring more uninvited sculptures to the Boston Common. Polish community leaders pleaded with city officials to keep it in Boston permanently, 'a fitting reminder of all Boston residents that freedom is not a privilege which is easily won,' one wrote. Beacon Hill aestheticians fulminated over 'such a wreck blighting our landscape' and implored the city to haul it away.

Over the years the debate sucked in everyone from Senate President William M. Bulger to the proprietor of a Polish restaurant to park rangers and tourists." (The Boston Globe, Wangsness, B1, B4, 1/20/2006)

Meanwhile, at least two groups in Boston are also working to keep "Partisans" in Boston. A South Boston arts group has contacted state Representative Brian P. Wallace, a Democrat from the neighborhood, to see whether he could help them find a place for the sculpture. South Boston has historically been home to a large sector of the city's Polish community." (The Boston Globe, Wangsness, B1, 1/26/2006)

Boston State House - Outside
BRONZES & STONES

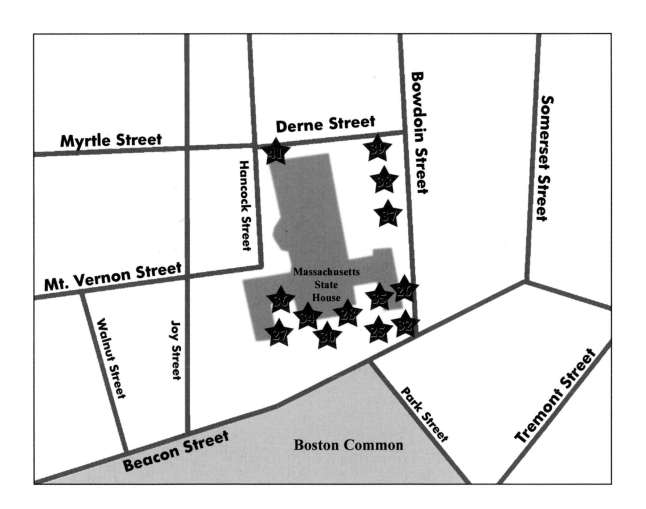

FRIGATE ARBELLA

Outside Boston State House south lawn
Bronze Plaque

To commemorate the arrival on June 12, 1630 of the
Frigate Arbella, bringing Governor Winthrop and
The Charter of the Massachusetts Bay Colony,
This tablet placed by the Massachusetts
Daughters of the American Revolution
Taken from the Bronze

A tiny bronze plaque for a colossal historic event.

GRAND ARMY

Outside Beacon Hill State House south lawn
Bronze Plaque 1930

"In 1868, Commander-in-Chief John A. Logan issued General Order No. 11 calling for all Departments and Posts to set aside the 30th of May as a day for remembering the sacrifices of fallen comrades, thereby beginning the celebration of Memorial Day." (http://surcw.org/gar.htm Dec. 28, 2010.)

Thus began the birth of our Memorial Day Weekend, Boston, MA.

HENRY CABOT LODGE (1850 –1924)

Outside Beacon Hill State House
Raymond A. Porter, Sculptor
Bronze / Stone
Statesman and Scholar

A public servant of Boston, rooted in generations of his Massachusetts family.

Beyond the West Wing of the State House stands a bronze statue of Henry Cabot Lodge (1850-1924), a Republican member of the House of Representatives from 1886 until 1893, and United States Senator from 1893 until his death over thirty years later. Although remembered chiefly as the implacable foe of Woodrow Wilson and the League of Nations, Lodge after being graduated from Harvard College and the Law School received in 1876 the first Ph.D. in political science awarded by the university, helped edit the North American Review, and wrote four historical biographies. His statue by Raymond A. Porter was commissioned by the Commonwealth to commemorate his services in Congress. At the dedication on 26 October 1932, David I. Walsh, Lodge's sometime colleague and successor in the Senate, delivered the oration. A walk from Beacon Street leads in to the Lodge statue.(Whitehill 104).

As a finale to his legacy of public service, Lodge made this speech in Symphony Hall prior to an election:
I love every inch of the old State, from the rocks of Essex and the glittering sands of the Cape to the fair Valley of the Connecticut and the wooded Berkshire Hills. Here my people have lived before me since the graveyards of Essex, on Boston Common, beneath the shadows of Park Street Church. Here I have lived all my life. To her service I have given my all: no man can give more. Others may easily serve her better than I in those days yet to be; but of this I am sure: that no one can ever serve her with a greater love or deeper loyalty. (Forbes and Eastman, quoting Lodge, 68 - 69).

DANIEL WEBSTER (1859)

Outside Beacon Hill State House / South lawn, Beacon Street
Hiram Powers (1805-1873), Sculptor
Bronze/Granite

Daniel Webster is shown in his stance as a powerful orator, arguing on behalf of our Union.

In 1816 Webster moved to Boston and became one of the nation's leading attorneys. His participation in the Dartmouth College case and McCulloch v. Maryland left an enormous imprint on American constitutional law. Webster also matured into one of the great orators of his era, delivering notable speeches at the bicentennial of the founding of Plymouth in 1820 and the dedication of the Bunker Hill Monument in 1825.

Webster was elected to Congress from Massachusetts in 1822 and served in the Senate from 1827 to 1841. During these years he underwent a political transformation, deserting his earlier free trade principles for strong support of the tariff. Webster had come to equate protectionism with the national interest.

In 1830, in one of the greatest exchanges in Senate history, Webster opposed nullification and argued for the supremacy of the federal government (Webster Hayne Debate). Webster and Andrew Jackson were united in their opposition to nullification, but disagreed on most other matters.

Webster yearned for the presidency, but failed to reach that ultimate goal -- a disappointment he shared with such other great contemporaries as John C. Calhoun and Henry Clay. As Secretary of State under William Henry Harrison and John Tyler, Webster negotiated the Webster-Ashburton Treaty in 1843, his greatest diplomatic achievement.

From 1845 to 1850, Webster served again in the Senate where he worked on behalf of the Compromise of 1850. Webster was personally opposed to slavery, but accommodated Southern concerns because of his deeply held belief that the preservation of the Union was more important than any other issue. This position cost him the support of anti-slavery groups in the North. From 1850 until his death, Webster was secretary of state under Millard Fillmore.

Daniel Webster (1782-1852) was canonized in bronze even more promptly than Mayor Quincy, for a Webster Memorial Committee undertook to obtain a statue of him soon after his death. The commission was awarded to the Vermont-born Hiram Powers (1805-1873), who had migrated to Florence in 1837.

"His first attempt, shipped from Leghorn in 1857, was lost at sea, but a second Webster statue reached Boston safely in 1859 and was placed on the terraced lawn in front of the State House. So the practice of pairing local worthies on pedestals in front of public buildings, begun at City Hall in 1856, was extended to the State House. Although Hiram Powers's statue, which depicted the subject in tail coat and trousers, without benefit of toga, had its critics, Nathaniel Hawthorne considered that, 'the face is very grand, very Webster.'" (Whitehill, 27)

Young Hiram, sculptor, migrated to Ohio with his family about 1818 to escape a famine in Vermont. Working odd jobs, Powers became a supervisor at a Cincinnati museum, where he learned to model clay. He traveled East, soliciting portrait bust commissions so successfully that Presidents Jackson and Calhoun, as well as Daniel Webster all sat for him.

Horace Mann (1796-1859)

Outside Beacon Hill State House
Miss Emma Stebbins (1815 – 1882), Sculptor
Bronze

Horace Mann was a lawyer, Massachusetts Legislator, Secretary of the State Board of Education, Congress man to the United States House of Representatives, President of Antioch College, and Promoter of Public Educational Reforms for Massachusetts.

My mentor, along with many other American public school teacher, I went to his teacher's schools. I attended the teaching schools of Salem State and University of Massachusetts, both of which are descendants of the "Normal Schools" founded by Horace Mann.

Horace Mann once said: "In a republic, ignorance is a crime. If we do not prepare children to become good citizens - if we do not develop their capacities, if we do not enrich their minds with knowledge - then our republic must go down to destruction." (O'Connor, 179)

"Webster gained a companion on 4 July 1865 when a bronze statue of Horace Mann (1796-1859) was placed opposite him on the State House lawn. Beginning as a lawyer and Massachusetts legislator, Mann became Secretary of the State Board of Education upon its creation in 1837, serving until 1848, when he was elected to the seat in the United States House of Representatives vacated by the death of John Quincy Adams. From 1852 to 1859 Horace Mann was president of Antioch College at Yellow Springs, Ohio. Funds for his memorial were collected from Massachusetts school children and teachers in 1860, the year following his death; the statue was modeled in Rome by Miss Emma Stebbins (1815-1882) and cast in bronze in Munich. The sculptress veiled Mann's clothing in a voluminous mantle, producing what was not unreasonably described as 'a mass of bad drapery.'" (Whitehill, 28)

During this period he served in the Massachusetts State Legislature as a member of the House from 1827 to 1833, and then as a member of the Senate from 1833 to 1837. As President of the Senate during his final year in the legislature, he signed a significant education bill, which became law on April 20, 1837.

During his years of service as the new Secretary of Education, Horace Mann transformed the moribund school system in Massachusetts.

Arguing that universal public education was the best way to turn the nation's unruly children into disciplined, judicious republican citizens, Mann won widespread approval from modernizers, especially in his Whig Party, for building public schools. Most states adopted one version or another of the system he established in Massachusetts, especially the program for "normal schools" to train professional teachers. Mann has been credited by many education historians as the "Father of the Common School Movement".

JOSEPH HOOKER

Outside Beacon Hill State House
Daniel Chester French / Edmund C. Potter, Sculptors
Bronze / Stone

Commander of the Army of the Potomac.
Defeated by Lee at Chancellorsville on 2-4 May 1863.
Won the Famous Battle of Lookout Mountain and Missionary Ridge.
The Soldier is the work of Daniel Chester French (1850-1931)
The Horse of Edmund C. Potter Dedicated on June 25, 1903
Taken from the Stone

Major General Joseph Hooker, who as commander on the Army of the Potomac, was defeated by Lee at Chancellorsville in May 1863, despite a two-to-one superiority in numbers.

The Commonwealth appropriated funds in 1896 for the statue, dedicated on 25 June 1903. The man is the work of Daniel Chester French (1850-1931); the horse, of Edward C. Potter. Of this monument Charles Francis Adams (1835-1915), a Civil War brevet brigadier general, wrote: 'Never since it has been placed there have I passed by the front of the State House without feeling a sense of wrong and insult at the presence, opposite the head of Park Street, of the equestrian statue of Hooker. The statue I look upon as an opprobrium cast on every genuine Massachusetts man who served in the Civil War. Hooker in no way and in no degree represents the typical soldiership of the Commonwealth.' (Whitehill, 53)

During the spring of 1863, Hooker established a reputation as an outstanding administrator and restored the morale of his soldiers, which had plummeted to a new low under Burnside. Among his changes were fixes to the daily diet of the troops, camp sanitary changes, improvements and accountability of the quartermaster system, addition of and monitoring of company cooks, several hospital reforms, and an improved furlough system (one man per company by turn, 10 days each). Other orders addressed the need to stem rising desertion (one from Lincoln combined with incoming mail review, the ability to shoot deserters, and better camp picket lines), more and better drills, stronger officer training, and for the first time, combining the federal cavalry into a single corps. Hooker said of his revived army: " I have the finest army on the planet. I have the finest army the sun ever shone on. ...   If the enemy does not run, God help them. May God have mercy on General Lee, for I will have none."

Hooker's mission was first to protect Washington, D.C. and Baltimore and second to intercept and defeat Lee. Unfortunately, Lincoln was losing any remaining confidence he had in Hooker. When the general got into a dispute with Army headquarters over the status of defensive forces in Harpers Ferry, he impulsively offered his resignation in protest, which was quickly accepted by Lincoln and General-in-chief Henry W. Halleck. On June 28, three days before the climactic Battle of Gettysburg, Hooker was replaced by Maj. Gen. George Meade. Hooker received the thanks of Congress for his role at the start of the Gettysburg Campaign, but the glory would go to Meade.

ANNE HUTCHINS 1922

Outside Beacon hill State House / near west wing
Cyrus E. Dallin, Sculptor
Bronze / Granite

In front of the West and East wings of the State House are twentieth century memorials to seventeenth century strong-minded ladies, who grievously disturbed the peace of Boston in their time. Anne Hutchinson (1591-1643), who arrived in Boston in 1634, so vigorously expounded a 'covenant of grace' that she was within three years tried for 'traducing the ministers and their ministry' and banished from the church and colony. In 1638 she emigrated to Rhode Island, and in 1642 to Pelham Bay in the Bronx, where she was killed by Indians.

Cyrus E. Dallin (1861-1944) represented her standing, with her small daughter by her side, her left arm clasping a Bible to her breast, and her face uplifted. His bronze statue, given to the Commonwealth in 1922 by the Anne Hutchinson Memorial Association and the State Federation of Women's Clubs, was placed outside the West Wing that was added to the State House in 1914-17. (Whitehill, 97)

MARY DYER 1959

Outside Beacon Hill State House near east wing
Sylvia Shaw Judson, Sculptor
Bronze / Granite

Quaker
Witness for religious Freedom
Hanged on Boston Common
1660
'My Life not Availeth Me
In Comparison to the
Liberty of the Truth'
Taken from the Stone

A Chicagoan, Sylvia Shaw Judson attended the Art Institute of Chicago and then studied in Paris under Bordelle, Rodin's pupil. Her work is owned by the Museum of Modern Art, the Metropolitan Museum, and the Philadelphia Museum of Art.

Mary Dyer and her husband were among those settling in Rhode Island with Anne Hutchinson, although they later broke off and resettled in Newport.

Her first attempt to return to Boston as a Quaker resulted in immediate imprisonment, and only by the steadfast entreaties of her husband was she released on the stipulation that she immediately be removed from the Colony, under guard, and being allowed to speak to no one during the journey. In September of 1659, Mary returned with William Robinson, Marmaduke Stevenson and Nicholas Davis, knowing full well of her peril, but with equal intent "to look the bloody laws in the face."

The three were immediately apprehended by the authorities imprisoned, tried and banished upon pain of death. At their first trial before Governor Endecott, he said, "we have made many laws and endeavored in several ways to keep you from among us, but neither whipping nor imprisonment, nor cutting off ears, nor banishment upon pain of death, will keep you from among us. We desire not your death." Ignoring the edict the three were soon imprisoned once again and regarded as "rushing upon a fool's fate." On October 20th the prisoners were brought before the Court of Magistrates with the "implacable" Endecott presiding. All three were condemned to be hanged.

The Boston General Court felt that Quaker doctrine assaulted the "fundamentall trueths [sic]" of religion. By denying the trinity, Christ, and the holy scriptures, Quakers belief in the "inner light" as the primary basis of revelation ran against the grain of Puritan dogma, with its scripturally based relationships of master/slave, king/subject, and father/family. Mary Dyer was hanged 1660. Because of this act, King Charles II overturned the stern Puritanical laws of Massachusetts Bay Colony.

JOHN F. KENNEDY

Outside Beacon Hill State House south lawn
Isabel McIlvain (1943-), Sculptor
Bronze / Stone

This bronze statue of John F. Kennedy, the 35th President of the United States. Dedicated on May 29, 1990, was designed and sculpted by Isabel McIlvain and paid for by the contributions of private citizens.

John Fitzgerald Kennedy, also referred to as John F. Kennedy, JFK, John Kennedy or Jack Kennedy, was the 35th President of the United States. In 1960 he became the youngest man ever elected president of the United States. He served from 1961 until his assassination in 1963.

Kennedy represented the state of Massachusetts from 1947 to 1960, first as a member of the U.S. House of Representatives, and then, in the U.S. Senate. Kennedy, the Democratic candidate, was elected President of the United States in 1960, at age 43, against Republican candidate Richard Nixon in one of the closest elections in American history at that time. He was assassinated on November 22, 1963.

MASSACHUSETTS FALLEN FIREFIGHTERS MEMORIAL 2007

Outside Beacon Hill State/ Bowdoin St. and Ashburton PL.
Robert Shure, Sculptor
Bronze

In this strong bronze pyramid, the artist depicts the constant war between man and fire as three firemen are positioned to fight a fire from every direction.

Efforts to construct a memorial to fallen firefighters began in 2000 with the formation of a non-profit association. After seven years of fund-raising and planning, this memorial was unveiled. Its design features three elements: the central bronze figures, a Ring of Honor consisting of bricks inscribed with the names of deceased firefighters, and the Firefighters' Prayer and Bell, placed to the side of the figures and ring. Sculptor Robert Shure also designed the Boston Irish Famine Memorial, located near Downtown Crossing, and a Korean War memorial in Charlestown Navy Yard. (http://www.publicartboston.com/content/massachusetts-fallen-firefighters) Nov. 27, 2010)

BEACON HILL MEMORIAL COLUMN

Outside Beacon Hill State House / Rear
Charles Bulfinch, Sculptor
Bronze / Granite

Clearly another first for Boston. This monument was the first in the country to honor our Revolutionary war heroes.

Created by Charles Bulfinch, architect of the State House, the Beacon Hill Memorial Column was originally erected in 1790, but removed in 1811. The memorial was recreated in 1990 and contains inscription plaques from the original monument. (http://www.ehow.com/list_7447995_monuments-capitol-ground-massachusetts.html Nov. 27, 2010).

The Beacon Monument dedicated to the fallen of The American Revolution was blown down 1789, the same year Charles Bulfinch, who graduated Harvard 1781, was chosen one of the selectmen of the town of Boston who redesigned the Beacon Hill Column. (Sentry 65 - 69).

DERNE STREET

Outside Beacon Hill State House / Rear
Slate plaque by John B. Hegnauer, 1992.
Presented by the George B. Henderson Foundation, 1992.

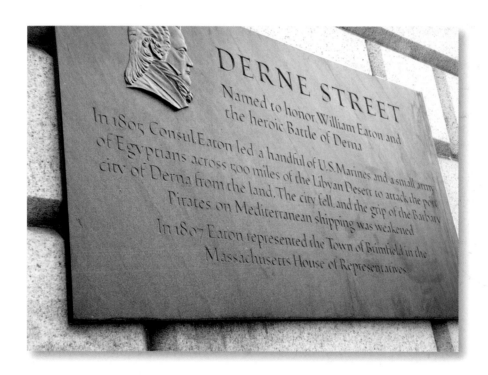

The city of Derne was Americas' first foreign conquered territory. In May 1804, William Eaton was given the commission of a navy lieutenant and sent back to the Barbary regencies, under the supervision of Commodore James Barron, to find Hamet Caramanli, a pasha, and enlist his cooperation in the war. Eaton found Caramanli in Alexandria and signed an agreement with him, although it is unclear if he had the authority to do so.

This contract, which was forwarded to Secretary of State Madison, specified that the United State would provide cash, ammunition and provisions for Hamet Caramanli's re-installation as pasha. It also designated William Eaton as "General and Commander in Chief" of the land forces that were to be used to carry out the operation.

The agreement defined the relationship between Caramanli and Eaton as well as their mission, but was never ratified by the United States Senate.

Sources do not always agree on the make up of Eaton's forces, but Spencer Tucker, biographer of Stephen Decatur, said that he had with him "ten Americans, three hundred Arab horsemen, seventy Christian mercenaries, and one thousand camels." The ten Americans including eight marines and two navy midshipmen.

It was with that force that Eaton and Caramanli made the 600 mile trek from Alexandria to Derne, a coastal city within the realm of Tripoli. By the time the band had reached the Gulf of Bomba, they had eaten their last rations and the Arab factions were on the verge of mutiny. Eaton had written to Captain Isaac Hull of the USS Argus requesting that the ship meet them there with supplies, but when they arrived on April 15, there was no ship to be seen. The next day, however, the Argus appeared as Hull had seen the smoke from their fires. After resupplying, they continued their journey, and on April 27, 1805, Eaton's forces attacked and took control of Derne.

Captain Presley O'Bannon of the U.S. Marine Corps raised the American flag for the first time over a conquered foreign city. At the Battle of Derne, one marine was killed and two were wounded. Eaton was wounded in the left wrist.

Twice Yusef Caramanli's, Hamets brother, forces tried and failed to take back the city. With the bey of Derne on the run and Hamet Caramanli reestablished in Derne, Eaton thought to march toward Tripoli. He requested reinforcements from Barron but instead received word that U.S. Consul-General Tobias Lear was negotiating peace with Yusef Caramanli. Then he received word from Lear himself that he was to surrender Derne as peace had been reached on June 4. The terms of the treaty required the U.S. to pay $60,000 for the release of the crew of the Philadelphia. Hamet Caramanli and his entourage of about 30 were allowed to leave, but his wife and family were held captive until 1807, as provided in the treaty.

Things haven't changed much on the Barbary Coast and Red Sea, even in our modern times.

SITE OF FIRST ENGLISH HIGH SCHOOL

Outside Beacon Hill State House / Rear / Derne St.
Bronze plaque Charles O. Crawford, 1924.
Given by the English High School Class of 1874.

This bronze marker is an example of an artistic bronze relief celebrating another first in Boston as well as in North America. Although not a free standing monument, this bronze speaks artistically of a first in American educational history.

The English High School of Boston, Massachusetts is the first public high school in America, founded in 1821. Originally called The English Classical School, it was renamed The English High School upon its first relocation in 1824.

The school is currently located in the Jamaica Plain area of Boston, its seventh location in the city. Its first location, located on Derne Street at the rear of the Massachusetts State House, is marked by a metal plaque. Its second location (still standing), on the corner of Pickney and Anderson Streets, eventually became the Phillips School, a school for then free-born and emancipated African Americans before the American Civil War. From 1844 to 1922, Boston English was a next-door neighbor of the Boston Latin School, first near downtown Boston and then in a building on Warren Street (now demolished) in the South End. From 1954 to 1989, it was located across the street from Boston Latin at 77 Avenue Louis Pasteur, the location is now part of the Harvard Medical School. Like Boston Latin, English only admitted boys for the first 151 years of its history and did not become coeducational until 1972. The current motto of the school is "College For All".

English High was created originally to educate working class schoolboys in preparation for business, mechanics, and engineering trades as opposed to "latin-grammar" schools like Boston Latin that prepared schoolboys for the college, ministry and scholarly pursuits, and private academies that were open only to affluent residents. Its original curriculum consisted of such courses as English, surveying, navigation, geography, logic, and civics as well as a strong emphasis on mathematics. Nowadays, English High has opened up its curriculum to include more liberal arts subjects such as foreign languages and writing as well as performing arts and more college preparatory courses.

Boston State House - Inside
BRONZES & STONES

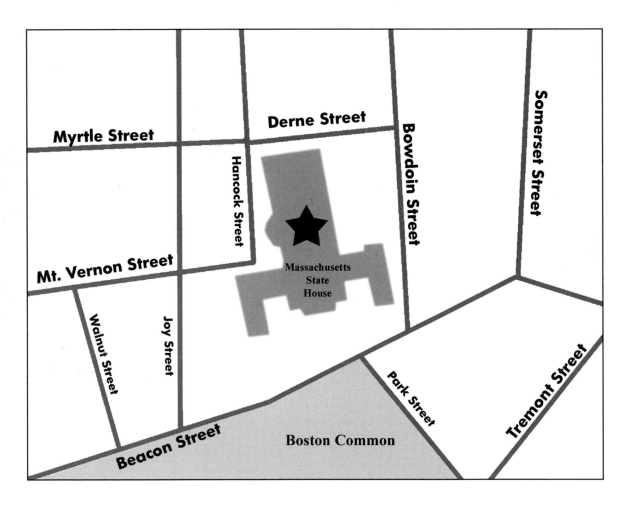

Myrtle Street

Derne Street

Bowdoin Street

Somerset Street

Hancock Street

Mt. Vernon Street

Massachusetts
State
House

Walnut Street

Joy Street

Park Street

Tremont Street

Beacon Street

Boston Common

All the artwork in this section is located inside the State House.
located on Beacon Street at Park Street

CHARLES BULFINCH

Inside Beacon Hill State House
Bronze plaque by Herbert Adams, 1899
Commissioned by the Commonwealth.

Bulfinch's first building was the Hollis Street Church (1788). Among his other early works are a memorial column on Beacon Hill (1789), the first monument to the American Revolution; the Federal Street Theater (1793); the "Tontine Crescent" (built 1793–1794, now demolished), fashioned in part after John Wood's Royal Crescent; the Old State House in Hartford Connecticut (1796); and the Massachusetts State House (1798).

Over the course of ten years, Bulfinch built a remarkable number of private dwellings in the Boston area, including Joseph Barrell's Pleasant Hill (1793), a series of three houses in Boston for Harrison Gray Otis (1796, 1800, 1806), and the John Phillips House (1804). He built several churches in Boston, of which New North Church (built 1802–1804), currently the Saint Stephens Church, is the last standing.

Serving from 1791 to 1795 on Boston board of selectmen, he resigned due to business pressures but returned in 1799. From 1799 to 1817 he was the chairman of Boston's board of selectmen continuously, and served as a paid Police Superintendent, improving the city's streets, drains, and lighting. Under his direction, both the infrastructure and civic center of Boston were transformed into a dignified classical style. Bulfinch was responsible for the design of the Boston Common, the remodeling and enlargement of Faneuil Hall (1805), and the construction of India Wharf. In these Boston years he also designed the Massachusetts State Prison (1803); Boylston Market (1810); University Hall for Harvard University (1813–1814); the Meeting House in Lancaster, Massachusetts (1815–17); and the Bulfinch Building of Massachusetts General Hospital (1818), its completion overseen by Alexander Paris, who was working in Bulfinch's office at the time the architect was summoned to Washington.

Despite this great activity and civic involvement, Bulfinch was insolvent several times starting in 1796, including at the start of his work on the statehouse, and was jailed for the month of July 1811 for debt (in a prison he had designed himself). There was no payment for his services as selectman, and he received only $1,400 for designing and overseeing the construction of the State House.

In the summer of 1817, Bulfinch's roles as selectman, designer and public official coincided with a visit by President Monroe. The two men were almost constantly in each other's company for the week-long visit, and a few months later (1818) Monroe appointed Bulfinch the successor to Benjamin Henry Latrobe (1764–1820) as Architect of the Capitol in Washington,D.C. (The Capitol Building had been partially burned by the British in 1814.) In this position he was paid a salary of $2,500 per year plus expenses.

As Commissioner of Public Building, Bulfinch completed the Capitol's wings and central portion, designed the western approach and portico, and constructed the Capitol's original low wooden dome to his own design (replaced by the present cast-iron dome in the mid-1850s). In 1829 Bulfinch completed the construction of the Capitol, 36 years after its cornerstone was laid. During his interval in Washington, Bulfinch also drew plans for the State House in Augusta, Maine (1829–32). He returned to Boston in 1830, where he died on April 15, 1844, aged 80, and was buried in Kings Chapel Burial Ground in Boston. His tomb was later moved to Mount Auburn in Cambridge, MA.

GEORGE WASHINGTON

Inside Beacon Hill State House
Sir Frances Chantrey, Sculptor
Carrara Marble

"The first significant Boston statue, completed on the fiftieth anniversary of independence in 1826, was inevitably of General George Washington." (Whitehill, 18)

Even after the American Revolution the United States still lacked the talent and schooling to have one of its own carve their first President. America subcontracted to Mother England, Sir Frances Chantrey did the deed with English monarchy garbs in mind.

The Doric Hall contains portraits, statues, and military artifacts recalling many periods of Massachusetts history. The 1826 this marble statue of George Washington by Sir Frances Chantrey was the first to be placed in the State House's Doric Hall. The statue was not entirely well received as many people at the time viewed the toga and noble stance was too royal for a nation that recently gained its independence from a monarchy. To solve the problem, it was decided that the statue depicts Washington rallying his troops at Valley Forge and that the toga is, actually a blanket as the event took place in December. The change apparently did the trick." (http://www.flickr.com/photos/22280677@N07/4749013815/ Nov. 27, 2010)

CURTIS GUILD

Inside Beacon Hill State House
Richard Recchia, Sculptor
John Evans & Company, fabricator, Cram and Ferguson, architectural firm.
Done 1915 - Numidian marble and Istrian marble.

CURTIS GUILD/1860-1915/CITIZEN OF BOSTON/A SOLDIER IN THE WAR/WITH SPAIN. LIEUTENANT/ GOVERNOR AND GOVERNOR OF THE COMMONWEALTH/SPECIAL AMBASSADOR TO/MEXICO AND AMBASSADOR/TO RUSSIA. TRUE SERVANT/OF MASSACHUSETTS AND/OF THE UNITED STATES

Taken from the Stone

An exemplary Bostonian public servant, Curtis Guild, Jr. was born in Boston, Massachusetts on February 2, 1860 to a prominent family n the journalism business. The Guild family was descended from John Guild and Elizabeth Crooke, early immigrants to the Boston area. His father, Curtis Guild, Sr., published the Commercial Bulletin, was a supporter of the arts, and served as president of the Bostonian Society.

Guild attended Harvard College. After graduation from college, Guild worked for his father's newspaper. Guild served as a member of the Massachusetts House of Representatives in 1881.

In 1891, Guild joined the Massachusetts Volunteer Militia, earning the rank of Brigadier General by 1898. During the Spanish American War he served as Inspector General of Havana.

In 1903, Guild was elected to serve as Lieutenant Governor in the administrations of John L. Bates and William Douglas. He was elected Governor for three terms, beginning in 1905 and served in that capacity from 1906 until 1909. (Curtis Guild, Jr. (February 2, 1860 - April 6, 1915) was the 43rd Governor of Massachusetts in the United States. He served from 1906 to 1909.

JOHN ADAMS / BUST

Inside Beacon Hill State House
Bronze bust by John F. Paramino, 1924, Sculptor
Replica of the original at New York University. Given by the Sons of the Revolution, 1925.

"I am determined in the meantime to be no longer the Dupe, and run in to Debt to support a vain post which has answered no other End than to make me unpopular." - John Adams, the second President of The United States.

Repeatedly, Adams would curse this above refrain throughout his political career.

Adams served three years as ambassador to Great Britain before returning to the United States in 1787 to become George Washington's first vice-president under the terms of the new Constitution.

Previously, Adams defended the British troops embroiled in the Boston Massacre incident when no other attorney would defend their rights in a court of law. Always his own man, with his own strong and stubborn views, John Adams clashed with Secretary of State Thomas Jefferson over questions of national policy, as well as with Secretary of the Treasury Alexander Hamilton, a member of his own Federalist party, over foreign policy issues.

"After Washington completed two terms in office, in 1796 John Adams was elected President of the United States, although he had to accept Thomas Jefferson as his vice-president. The most important controversy of his administration came with his fellow Federalist, Alexander Hamilton, over the question of war with France. Relations between the United States and France had deteriorated so badly that French and American ships were already firing on one another on the high seas. Although Hamilton and his supporters argued strongly in favor of a declaration of war, Adams stubbornly held out for a peaceful settlement. To Adams's good fortune, Napoleon Bonaparte came to power in 1799 and agreed to peaceful negotiations with the United States." (Eminent Bostonians, O'Connor, 7)

HONOR OF ALL VETERANS

Inside Beacon Hill State House
Emilius R. Ciampa, Sculptor
Bronze Plaque

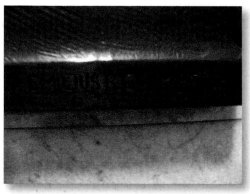

In honor off all veterans who served in the Armed Services of the United States in the first world war to preserve democracy and freedom. The Commonwealth of Massachusetts erects this tribute and records the peoples prayer for lasting liberty and peace.
Taken from the Bronze

NELSON APPLETON MILES (1931)

Doric Hall / Boston State House
John Francis Paramino, Sculptor
Bronze Plaque

NELSON APPLETON MILES
A SOLDIER SON OF MASSACHUSETTS
CIVIL WAR
AWARDED A CONGRESSIONAL MEDAL OF HONOR BRIGADIER
AND BREVET MAJOR GENERAL UNITED STATES
INDIAN WARS
COLONEL FIFTH REGIMENT UNITED STATES INFANTRY
BRIGADIER GENERAL UNITED STATES
SPANISH AMERICAN WAR
MAJOR GENERAL COMMANDING THE ARMY LIEUTENANT
GENERAL BY SPECIAL ACT OF CONGRESS JUNE 6, 1900
A GRATEFUL COMMONWEALTH HAS ERECTED THIS TABLET
IN COMMEMORATION OF HIS DISTINGUISHED"
Taken from the Bronze

WAR NURSES, 1911

Inside Beacon Hill State House
Bela Pratt / Sculptor
Bronze / Granite

With its tender caress, the sculptured War Nurses rightfully represent all nurses, in all wars, a moving masterpiece.

Built largely of Pavonazzo marble this room houses Nurses' Hall because of the statue of an Army war nurse located here. Sculpted in 1914 by Bela Pratt, it was the first statue erected in honor of the women of the North after the Civil War.

Pratt traveled to Paris, where he trained with sculptors Henri-Michel-Antoine Chapu(1833-1891) and Alexandre Falguière .

In 1892, he returned to the United States to create two large sculptural groups representing *The Genius of Navigation* for the World's Columbian Exposition in Chicago. He also produced sculptures for the Pan-American Exposition at Buffalo in 1901. In 1893, he began a 25-year career as an influential teacher of modeling in the School of the Museum of Fine Arts, Boston.

During this time, Pratt sculpted a series of busts of Boston's intellectual community, including Episcopal priest Phillips Brooks (1899, Brooks House, Harvard University), Colonel Henry Lee (1902, Memorial Hall, Harvard University), and Boston Symphony Orchestra founder Henry Lee Higginson (1909, Symphony Hall, Boston).

He became an associate of the National Academy in 1900.

When Saint-Gaudens' uncompleted group for the entrance to the Boston Public Library was rejected, Pratt was awarded a commission for personifications of Art and Science. Pratt continued Saint-Gaudens' influence in coin design after 1907. His gold Indian Head half ($5) and quarter ($2.50) eagles are known as the "Pratt coins" and feature an unusual intaglio Indian head, the U.S. mint's only recessed design in circulation. A retrospective exhibition of 125 of his sculptures was held at the Museum of Fine Arts, Boston in the spring of 1918.

CLARA BARTON

Inside Beacon Hill State House
Robert Shure, Sculptor
Bronze Plaque

Clara Barton was born on December 25, 1821 Oxford, Massachusetts.

Clara Barton founded the American Red Cross foundation. She also became a teacher at the age of seventeen and founded her own school which she wasn't elected to teach in. The board of directors hired a man instead of her. Clara Barton then thought that she should be paid as much as any man should for the same amount of work. Although many today think she has the right idea, there is still a problem of uneven salaries in today's society.

Her nickname in the Civil War was the Angel of the Battlefield.

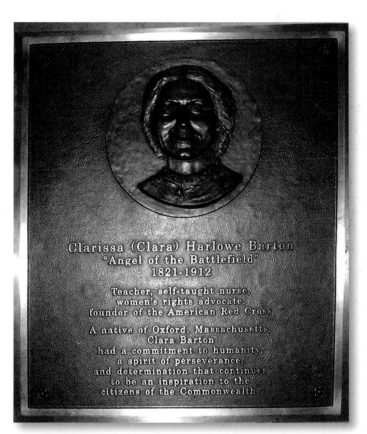

LAWRENCE AND ROBERT WASHINGTON

Inside Beacon Hill State House / Doric Hall
Sandstone facsimiles of ancestral tombstones of George Washington, c. 1860.
Commissioned by Earl Spencer of Apthorp and given to the Commonwealth
through Senator Charles Sumner, 1861.

Donated reproductions of George Washington's English decedents stone markers, from Charles Sumner.

The lower right stone depicts the Washington family coat of arms.

The upper left stone indicates the lineage genealogy of the Washington family roots connected to the British Spencer's family, the royal family of Princess Diana.

JOHN HANCOCK

Inside Beacon Hill State House / Doric Hall
Bronze portrait bust and commemorative plaque cast by the John Williams Foundry, 1915
The bust is cast from the marble statue of Hancock by Horatio Stone at the U. S. Capitol, Washington, DC.
Given by the Massachusetts Society Sons of the Revolution, 1915.

A merchant, patriot, almost commander of the Continental Army and leader of his home state of Massachusetts John Hancock is a true American hero.

"So King George can read my name without spectacles," said John Hancock at the signing of the Declaration of Independence.

John Hancock was the first Governor Of Massachusetts after the Revolution. His family mansion would become the new Beacon Hill State House 1780.

If three members of the Massachusetts House of Representatives had reversed their votes in 1859, the Hancock Mansion, known also as the Old Stone House, would probably now remain standing near No. 25 Beacon Street, a more beautiful and more fitting monument to our First Governor than his statue which is in the State House.

The Hancock mansion descended to a nephew and namesake of the Governor and his will, made two years previously, contained this clause: 'I direct that the Mansion House on Beacon Street shall not be sold till four years after my decease, and that the sale of the same shall be advertised in one or more papers in Boston, New York, Philadelphia and Washington. I hope the estate may not be sold, but retained in the family, but if sold, I direct that it not be sold in one lot, it be sold in four separate lots, and if sold in four separate lots, that the house be sold separately,' Governor Banks recommended that the State acquire the property, but always some complication prevented it.

In the same year, 1859, a joint Special Committee headed by Edward G. Baker recommended the purchase of the property 'as the great New England monument of the Revolution,' declaring it to be 'the Mount Vernon of New England.'

In 1863 when it was proposed to demolish the Mansion a Committee of the City Council, of which Thomas C. Amory, Jr. was the Chairman, urged the City to accept the offer of the heirs, headed by Charles L. Hancock, to donate the house so that it could be reconstructed on some appropriate location. Had the City carried out the suggestion the 'Mansion' might now be standing on one of the situations recommended by the Committee, on the northerly corner of Newbury and Clarendon Streets, now the home of the New England Mutual Life Insurance Company. Two years after Hancock's death his heirs sold the land upon which the State House now stands.

A tablet formerly placed at the North-West gate of the State House, but since removed, indicated the approximate location of the entrance to the dwelling. The location today, according to an old survey dated November 1815, would be about thirty-five feet back from Beacon Street on the lawn in front of the West wing of the State House about midway between the entrance path to the West wing and the American Unitarian Association Building now numbered 25 Beacon Street but originally numbered 32. At the time the estate covered approximately the lands bounded by Beacon, Bowdoin, Joy and Mt. Vernon Streets, about seven acres in all.

Hancock's entry into Philadelphia to attend the Provincial Congress was spectacular.

His part in the Revolution, and his Governorship of the State have been enlarged upon by many writers. He will go down in history as one of our greatest patriots.

It may be of interest to note that there was a street known as Hancock Avenue that ran from Beacon Street to Mount Vernon Street. The location was about where the entrance path to the West Wing of the State House is now located. The main street in Quincy, the town of his birth, is also named for him.

While serving as Governor, John Hancock on June 22, 1792 signed the charter of the Union Bank which in September 1925, as the National Union Bank, was merged with the State Street Trust Company. This charter is one of the prized items in our historical collection." (Forbes and Eastman, 55, 56 and 59)

WILLIAM FRANCIS BARTLETT 1901

Inside Beacon Hill State House
Daniel Chester French, Sculptor
Bronze

Daniel Chester French's work is highly attentive to detail -- anatomically as well as in the folds of his subjects clothes. French is America's answer to Italy's Bernini.

"Daniel Chester French's bronze of Major General William Francis Bartlett saluting the colors, having been intended, by act of 1901, for the State House grounds, avoided similar deportation only because in 1903 the Governor and Council voted that it be placed indoors, in Memorial Hall with the Civil War battle flags, where it still is. Bartlett, born in 1840, volunteered at the outbreak of the war, was a major general at the age of twenty-four, and died in 1876. He is a handsome figure." (Whitehill, 59)

Bartlett was born in Haverhill, Massachusetts attended Phillips Academy in Andover, Massachusetts and entered Harvard College in 1858. The Civil War began during his junior year and, almost immediately after hearing of the surrender of Fort Sumter, Bartlett enlisted as a private with the Massachusetts Volunteer Militia.

Bartlett initially enlisted in the 4th Battalion Massachusetts Infantry, also known as the New England Guards, which was garrisoned to defend Fort Independence.

During the siege at Yorktown, Virginia on April 24, 1862, Capt. Bartlett was shot in the knee by Confederate pickets. The wound required the amputation of his leg. Bartlett returned to Boston to recuperate and, during the summer of 1862, finished his degree at Harvard.

One of the most wounded and heroic Union soldiers of the American Civil War. During one of several assaults on Port Hudson on May 27, 1863, Bartlett was shot twice—once in his other leg and another hit that shattered his wrist. These wounds effectively removed him from command until the end of the 49th's term of service in September 1863. Bartlett resigned his commission on September 1, 1863.

While still recuperating from his wounds received in Louisiana, Bartlett began to organize, in the fall of 1863, another regiment. This unit, the 57th Massachusetts Infantry was one of four "Veteran Regiments," organized in Massachusetts to consist almost exclusively of men who had already served out an enlistment with a previous regiment. Bartlett was placed in command of the 57th regiment. Early in the campaign, Bartlett was again wounded, this time in the head, during the Battle of The Wilderness on May 6, 1864. He returned to Massachusetts and, while recovering, received a promotion to brigadier general.

ROGER WOLCOTT 1900

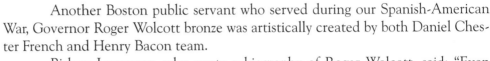

Inside Beacon Hill State House
Daniel Chester French / Henry Bacon, Sculptors
Bronze / Marble

Another Boston public servant who served during our Spanish-American War, Governor Roger Wolcott bronze was artistically created by both Daniel Chester French and Henry Bacon team.

Bishop Lawrence, who wrote a biography of Roger Wolcott, said: "Even before he opened his mouth, he had gained the interest and sympathy of the audience." Another friend made the remark, "He stood four-square to all the winds that blew."

In 1881 he was elected to the Massachusetts Legislature and later in 1892 he was chosen Lieutenant-Governor in a Democratic year when Cleveland became President and William E. Russell, Governor, and in 1896 he became Governor upon Greenhalge's death. In that year he swept every city, including Boston itself, and all towns in the State, except one, the greatest majority any Governor had received. He was twice returned to office, in 1897 and 1898.

Wolcott preferred to serve the State of which he was so fond, for at least twice he declined positions abroad. McKinley asked him to serve on a Philippine Commission, and he was also offered the Ambassadorship to Italy. He died in 1900, his funeral taking place the day before Christmas, all stores being closed although it was the best day of the year for shopping.

The untimely death in 1900 of Governor Roger Wolcott was so widely regretted that voluntary offerings from thousands of Massachusetts people poured in for a memorial to him. This took the form of a seated bronze portrait on the third floor of the State House opposite the main staircase. As he had been Governor during the Spanish-American War, the memorial also commemorates the Massachusetts men who served in that conflict. The statue is placed against an architectural background designed by Henry Bacon (who later designed the Lincoln Memorial in Washington), and is flanked by marble pilasters on which French carved figures representing the typical soldier and sailor of the war. It was dedicated on 31 December 1906. (Whitehill, 71)

JOHN ALBION ANDREW, 1870

Inside Beacon Hill State House / Doric Hall
Thomas Ball, Sculptor
Carrara Marble

In the spirit of our Massachusetts Minutemen during our Revolutionary War, characterized by preparedness, readiness; Gov. Andrews was the first governor of his country, to send the first troops to Washington D.C. during our Civil War.

John Albion Andrew (1818-1867), Civil War Governor of Massachusetts and one of the most effective supporters of the Union, died less than a year after his retirement from office. With the precedent of statues to commemorate Daniel Webster, Horace Mann, and Edward Everett, private citizens raised a subscription to procure a memorial that would show the affectionate regard of the people of Massachusetts for their late Governor. Thomas Ball, back from Italy on a visit, was asked to make a model for a statue in competition with several other artists. His design was chosen; the marble statue that was carved in 1870 was unveiled in Doric Hall at the State House on 14 February 1871. Although the statue is without classical embellishments, the folds of voluminous cloak attempt to mitigate the severity of contemporary costume, but fail to conceal a pair of very unpressed trousers.

From the year 1861 through 1865, Andrew was Governor of Massachusetts and proved to be one of the ablest and most effective of the so-called 'War Governors.' Such was his foresight and understanding of conditions that through his energetic efforts the militia regiments were rapidly recruited, well armed and trained, with the result that Massachusetts was the only northern state in any way prepared for war when Fort Sumter was fired upon. Troops were mustered in Boston the day after President Lincoln's call for volunteers and on the day following the 6th Massachusetts Volunteer Infantry started for the defense of Washington – the first fully armed and equipped volunteer regiment to reach the capital.

Andrew's name is included in the list of fifty-three noted men perpetuated upon the frieze of the House of Representatives in the Massachusetts State House.

Governor Andrew, of the Commonwealth of Massachusetts, at an impressive ceremony in the Hall of Flags at the State House, accepted the battle flags of the Massachusetts units when they were returned after the war, 'borne hither by surviving representatives of the same heroic regiments and companies to which they were entrusted.' As he so well stated. (Forbes and Eastman)

"Hear Us" — State House Women's Leadership Project

Inside Beacon Hill State House / second floor south, outside Doric Hall
Sheila Levrant de Bretteville and Susan Sellers / Robert Shure, Sculptors
Two-toned Marble.

In 1996, the Massachusetts legislature recognized that the State House art collection included only a handful of images of women. They recommended that a new work of art be created to honor the contributions of women to public life in Massachusetts. Now permanently installed on a large wall just outside Doric Hall, the work depicts six women selected by an advisory committee. Dorothea Dix (1802-87); Lucy Stone (1818-93); Sarah Parker Remond (1814-94); Josephine St. Pierre Ruffin (1842-1924); Mary Kenney O'Sullivan (1864-1943); and Florence Luscomb (1887-1985) were chosen to represent all the women who dedicated themselves to improving life in the Commonwealth. The two-toned marble panels designed by artists Sheila Levrant de Bretteville and Susan Sellers include words written by the women etched on the stone and bronze busts cast from period photographs. The portraits are by artist Robert Shure.

Beacon Hill & Louisburg Square
BRONZES & STONES

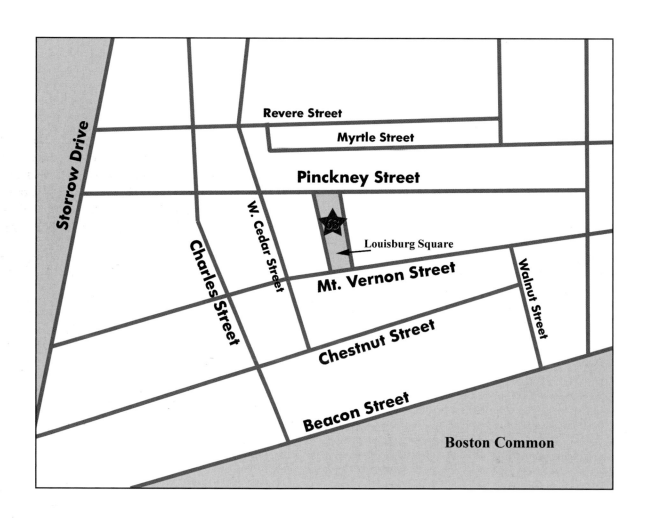

CHRISTOPHER COLUMBUS & ARISTIDES THE JUST

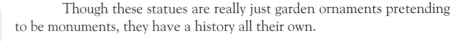

Louisburg Square, Beacon Hill
Unknown sculptor
Stone / Cement

Though these statues are really just garden ornaments pretending to be monuments, they have a history all their own.

In 1850 modest stone statues of Columbus and Aristides the Just appeared in the fenced garden of Louisburg Square on Beacon Hill as the gift to his fellow proprietors of Joseph Iasigi, a Greek merchant, who lived at number 3. They were brought from Leghorn in one of Iasigi's ships, possibly as ballast, possible in an unfulfilled hope of sale. These are not very remarkable works of art, nor did their subjects great-

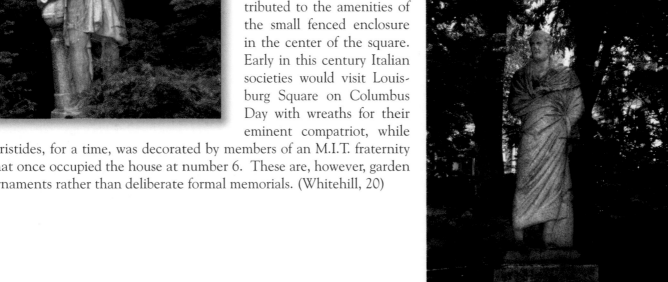

ly arouse general interest. With a fountain (now disappeared), they simply contributed to the amenities of the small fenced enclosure in the center of the square. Early in this century Italian societies would visit Louisburg Square on Columbus Day with wreaths for their eminent compatriot, while Aristides, for a time, was decorated by members of an M.I.T. fraternity that once occupied the house at number 6. These are, however, garden ornaments rather than deliberate formal memorials. (Whitehill, 20)

Boston Public Garden
BRONZES & STONES

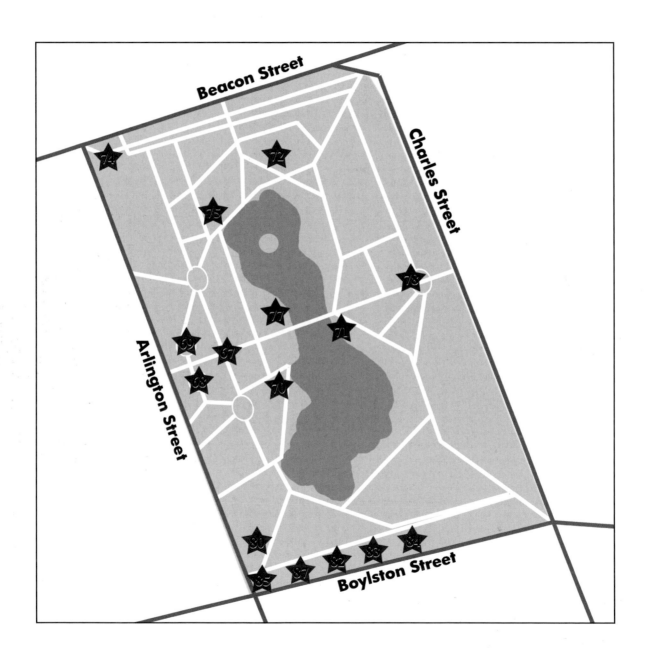

GEORGE WASHINGTON (1869)

Boston Public Gardens – Arlington St.
Thomas Ball (1819 -1911), Sculptor
Bronze/Stone

Sculptor Thomas Ball created this equestrian statue of George Washington which was cast, mounted, and dedicated in 1869. The statue's sword has been broken so often by vandals that it was finally replaced with fiberglass. The plaster study of it is on display in the Boston Atheneum Reading Room.

Since 1776, George Washington has been called The Father of Our Country by his fellow Americans. If there was an American Mount Olympus, Washington would be at the pinnacle.

Since the 1790s his image was everywhere -- on paintings, coins, prints, plates -- as well as seen here as a statute.

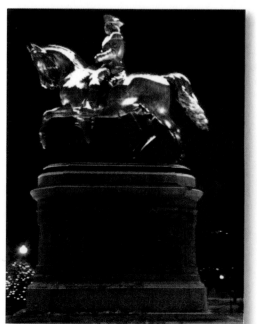

John Adams once said that George Washington had "the gift of taciturnity," meaning he had an instinct for the eloquent silence.

Here depicted as the resilient Military General of the American Revolution, not obsessed with winning battles but stead fast in his will to keep his Continental Army surviving and alive, wearing down the will of the British Army.

George Washington's strength, whether it be military or political, was in his ability to surrender his omnipotent power as a leader in both positions of leadership.

Washington began the tradition of a two-term presidency, national unity and the long standing policy of independence from foreign powers, Proclamation of Neutrality "the strategy of enlightened procrastination." (Ellis,127-131)

"BOY AND BIRD, 1934, RECAST 1977

Boston Public Gardens on Washington's left
Bashka Paeff (1893 - 1979), Sculptor
Bronze fountain, life size

A student of the renowned sculptor Bela Pratt, Paeff was born in Russia. She studied in Paris prior to the Boston Museum School

This tiny sculpture is an example of art-for-art's-sake, a beautiful bronze enhancing the beauty of the Boston Public Gardens. Sculptures such as these are designed to augment one's experience while walking through botanical gardens and are an asset wherever they are displayed.

SMALL CHILD

Boston Public Gardens / On Washington's statue right
Mary E. Moore (1887-1967), Sculptor
Bronze fountain

Like Bashka Paeff, Mary E. Moore studied under Bela Pratt. Moore was born in Taunton and taught at Beaver Country Day School in Brookline. The statue was given to the City of Boston by Mrs. Alfred Tozzer.

Pratt was a master sculptor and the work of his students which ornament the Boston Public Gardens carries on the Boston tradition of great art masters passing their knowledge and skill to those who come to study with them.

BAGHEERA, 1986

Fountain near swan boats / Boston Public Gardens
Lillian Swann Saarinen (1912 - 1995), Sculptor
Bronze / Granite

One of many whimsical sculptures ornamenting Boston Public Gardens.

Rudyard Kipling's *Jungle Books*, and the panther Bagheera, served as the inspiration for this charming sculpture. Friends of the sculptor, Lillian Swann Saarinen, with the cooperation of the Friends of the Public Garden, placed this sculpture in a Public Gardens fountain.

Lillian Swann attended The Pratt Institute where she studied under Carl Milles, Hein Warneke, and Alexander Archipenko. She also studied at Hunter College, the Arts Student League of New York, and the Cranbrook Academy in Michigan, where she met and married Eero Saarinen, who was destined to become one of the foremost architects of the twentieth century, creating "The Gateway to The West," Arch in St. Louis, Missouri.

Lillian Swann Saarinen was a resident of Boston and Cambridge. A portraitist and animalist, she won the Anna Hyatt Huntington prize, among others. She was a master in bronze, ceramic, porcelain and pottery mediums. She created pieces that are realistic and representational. An animal specialist, an art educator, teacher, lecturer and builder of public art monuments.

TRITON BABIES

Fountain near swan boats / Boston Public Gardens
Anna Coleman Watts Ladd, Sculptor
Bronze / Granite

Anna Coleman Watts Ladd (1878 – June 3, 1939) was an American sculptress in Manchester, Massachusetts, who devoted her time throughout World War I to soldiers who were disfigured.

She married Dr. Maynard Ladd, and there studied with Bela Pratt for three years at the Boston Museum School. Her Triton Babies piece was shown at the 1915 Panama-Pacific Exposition in San Francisco. (It is now a fountain sculpture in the Boston Public Garden.) In 1916 she was a founder of the Guild of Boston Artists, where she held a one-woman show.

Ladd challenged herself on many artistic fronts and wrote two books, *Hieronymus Rides*, based on a medieval romance she worked on for years, and *The Candid Adventurer*, a sendup of Boston society in 1913. She also wrote at least two unproduced plays, one of which incorporated the story of a female sculptor who goes to war.

She devoted herself to portraiture and was well regarded. Her portrait of Eleanora Duse was one of only three that the actress ever allowed. In late 1917, in Paris, Ladd founded the American Red Cross "Studio for Portrait-Masks" to provide cosmetic masks to be worn by men who had been badly disfigured in World War I.

Soldiers would come to Ladd's studio to have a cast made of their face and their features sculpted onto clay or plasticine. This form was then used to construct the prosthetic piece from extremely thin galvanized copper. The metal was painted to resemble the recipient's skin, and the prosthesis was donned with strings or eyeglasses.

The present day correlation to the work of Ladd is the field of anaplastology. This field is the art and science of restoring absent or malformed anatomy through artificial means.

MAKE WAY FOR DUCKLINGS (1987)

Boston Public Gardens
Nancy Schön, Sculptor
Bronze / Stone

This Sculpture has been placed here as a tribute to Robert McCloskey whose story "Make Way for Ducklings" has made the Boston Public Garden familiar to children through out the world. (1987)
Taken from the Bronze

Make Way for Ducklings, a children's book written by Robert McCloskey in 1941, won the Caldecott Medal (an award given annually for outstanding juvenile literature) in 1942. It quickly became a classic, going through seventeen printings and selling more than 700,000 copies. With his own drawings, McCloskey relates the tale of a pair of mallard ducks looking for a nesting site in Boston. They find the perfect place on an island in the Charles River Basin, but they remember the peanuts fed them by visitors to the Public Garden. When the ducklings are old enough, Mrs. Mallard and her progeny take a stroll up sidewalks and through traffic. One of Boston's newer traditions is a children's parade retracing the ducklings' route on Duckling Day (Mothers Day).

Requests for replicas in other cities have been turned down by the sculptor because 'it's a Boston story.' She made exception when Russian First Lady Raisa Gorbachev asked her American counterpart Barbara Bush for a duplicate for Moscow; in 1991 a duck family was installed in Gorky Park.

Dedicated in the 150th anniversary year of the Public Garden, the sculpture is considered a tribute to McCloskey, whose drawings the sculptor followed closely. Given to the City of Boston by Friends of the Public Garden.

Nancy Schön (born 1928) is a renowned sculptor of public art displayed internationally. Nancy prides herself in having work that is totally interactive. Her sculptures are available for people to touch, sit on, hug and interact with every day of the year, day or night.

Another major work by Nancy Schön's besides *Make Way for Ducklings* is *The Tortoise and Hare,* which is a metaphor for the Boston Marathon and is located at the finish line in Copley Square.

As Nancy creates a work of art, her research is a quest for knowledge and of understanding issues and of learning, including her philosophy of "reflection in action". "We learn so much from our inquiry but as my husband said, 'we know more than we can say' and I would always say back to him that I think our unconscious is brilliant!"

GEORGE ROBERT WHITE MEMORIAL BOSTON

Public Gardens / Corner Arlington / Beacon Streets
Daniel Chester French, Sculpture
Bronze / Granite

Cast Thy Bread Upon The Waters For Thou Shalt Find It
After Many Days - ECCLES XII
In Memory of George Robert White (1847 – 1922)
A Public Spirited Citizen Whose Great Gift to the City of Boston
Provided For the Creation of Works of Public Utility and
Beauty for the Use and Enjoyment of the Inhabitants.
Sculpted by Daniel Chester French
Erected in 1924
Henry Bacch was the Architect of the memorial
George Robert White born in Lynnfield, Massachusetts on July 19, 1847
Gave $1,000,000 to the Massachusetts College of Pharmacy and other
gifts to the Museum of Fine Arts to mention just a few.

Taken from the Stone

ETHER MONUMENT

Boston Pubic Gardens
Arlington St. / Beacon St.
John Quincy Adams Ward / Henry Van Brunt, Sculptors
Granite

Neither shall there be Anymore Pain. -- Rev.
To Commemorate the Discovery that the
Inhaling of Ether causes Insensibility to Pain."
First proved to the world at the Massachusetts
General Hospital in Boston
-- October AD MDCCCXLVI"
This also cometh Forth from the Lord of Hosts
which is wonderful in counsel and excellent in working.
-- Isaiah
The Gift of Thomas Lee in Gratitude for the
relief of Human Suffering by the inhaling of Ether.
A Citizen of Boston has erected this monument.
-- AD MDCCCLXVII
Ether Centennial Dedicated Oct. 16, 1946
Taken from the Stone

The Ether Centennial took place last autumn on October 16th, 1946; and as the monument
in the Public Garden to the 'discoverer of ether' has
been described in our booklet entitled Some Interesting Boston Events, this chapter is devoted chiefly
to the most appropriate remarks made at the centennial celebration by several leading medical authorities. Dr. Reginald Fitz recalled a number of incidents
and records relating to that first operation under the
Ether Dome of the Massachusetts General Hospital.
This room contains the inscription, part of which
reads, 'On October 16, 1846, in this room, then the
operating theatre of the Hospital, was given the first

public demonstration of anesthesia to the extent of producing insensibility to pain during a serious surgical operation.' Dr. Fitz referred to the diary of the surgeon of that first operation, Dr. J.C. Warren, which contained this entry written on the same day: 'Did an interesting operation at the Hospital this morning, while the Patient was under the influence of Dr. Morton's preparation to prevent pain. The substance employed was Sulphuric Ether.' On the day following the operation Dr. Warren wrote: 'I hereby certify that I have twice seen the administration of Dr. Morton's application for the prevention of pain; that it had a decided effect in preventing the sufferings of the patients during the operation and that no bad consequences resulted.' Some months afterwards Dr. Warren swore that he had never heard of ether in a surgical operation until Morton suggested it. When this famous surgeon resigned from the Medical School he made this statement: 'A discovery which every medical man, and especially every practical surgeon, must hail with unmingled satisfaction.'"

Another first-hand account was written by Edward Everett, President of Harvard University, whose diary is deposited in the Massachusetts Historical Society. The late Allyn B. Forbes, Director of that Society, very kindly sent us this information:

It appears from his diary that on the morning of October 16, 1846, when the first ether operation was going on, Everett was trying to get up a breakfast party for the next day. The first reference that he makes to ether is on November 3. In the evening he went to Dr. Bigelow's for an informal meeting of the American Academy. At that time, young Dr. Bigelow read an account of a stupefying gas prepared by Dr. Morton, a dentist, and inhaled by persons about to be operated upon. Dr. Morton had used it in many cases with entire success: -- nearly 200. It has also been used in the hospital in cases of ordinary surgery and generally with success. (Forbes and Eastman, 42)

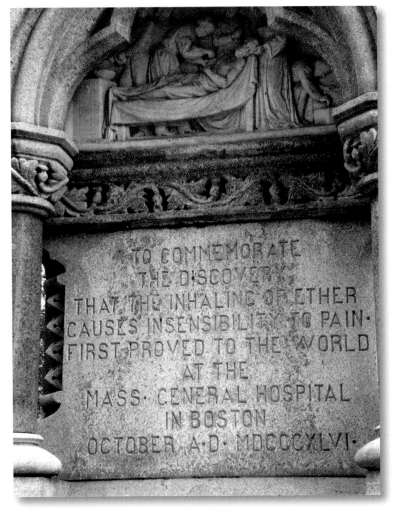

TO COMMEMORATE
THE DISCOVERY
THAT THE INHALING OF ETHER
CAUSES INSENSIBILITY TO PAIN·
FIRST PROVED TO THE WORLD
AT THE
MASS· GENERAL HOSPITAL
IN BOSTON
OCTOBER A·D· MDCCCXLVI·

JAPANESE LANTERN   (16TH CENTURY)

Boston Public Garden / near Bridge
Donated by Japanese Art Dealer Bunkio Matsuki
Iron / Granite

Ornamenting Boston's beautiful Public Gardens, this iron lantern was a gift from the people of Japan in 1904.

The lantern is symbolic of the light brought to gardens by other Japanese lanterns and was donated by Japanese art dealer Bunkio Matsuki. Since the 7th century such lanterns were used in Buddhist temples and shrines. Matsuki was born in Japan where he was trained as a Buddhist monk but he immigrated to Boston in 1888 where he established a business promoting Japanese art.

EDWARD EVERETT HALE

Boston Public Garden Charles St.
Bela Lyon Pratt (1867-1917), Sculptor
Bronze / Stone

Author of "Man without a Country."
Man of letters preacher of the Gospel prophet of peace patriot 1822-1909"
The incarnation of the spirit of Boston during the 19th century. Author of "Man Without a Country".
"If you seek his real monument you will find it in the hearts of the poor and oppressed" Mayor Fitzgerald of Boston
Statue unveiled 1913 by his grandson Edward Everett Hale in the presence of former President William Howard Taft.
Taken from the Stone

The robed Channing stands sedately in a niche opposite Arlington Street Church as a hieratic Unitarian saint; Bishop Brooks vigorously exhorts passersby in Copley Square; but the Reverend Edward Everett Hale (1822-1909), author, and Unitarian clergyman, is simply going for a walk in the Public Garden in civilian clothes, hat and stick in hand. This heroic size bronze statue, the result of a subscription among citizens, was the work of Bela Lyon Pratt (1867-1917), long a teacher of sculpture at the Museum of Fine Arts School. It was placed near the central entrance from Charles Street to the Public Garden in 1913 on so low a pedestal that Dr. Hale seems about to step down and start off for the miniature suspension bridge across the pond in the direction of Commonwealth Avenue." (Whitehill, 78)

Even if the passer-by believes the statue of Edward Everett Hale in the Public Garden is oversize, it may be a reminder to read or reread the two most talked about stories written by this well-known scholar, preacher, patriot, benefactor, author and philanthropist. He first became known as a writer in 1859 when the Atlantic Monthly published his story entitled, "My Double and How He Undid Me." *The Man Without a Country* appeared during the Civil War and undoubtedly advanced the loyalty of the Union. Both are similar in one respect; they are so persuasive they make most readers believe they are true incidents, reported accurately by the author. The account of Philip Nolan, the United States Navy officer who disowned his country and hoped he would never see or hear of the U.S.A. again and who was punished by banishment and never being allowed to hear the name of one's eyes, until the last page when the reader discovers it is all fiction.

This statue was unveiled in 1913 by his grandson Edward Everett Hale, his widow watching the ceremony from a carriage on Charles Street. Services were also held at the Unitarian Church. Ex-President William Howard Taft described Dr. Hale as a man of 'irresistible personality,' adding that 'His culture, his nobility, his oratory and his disposition all helped to gain him a just reputation which has made every individual in this country, whether of New England or not, proud that Edward Everett Hale was an American.' Hon. John D. Long said in part: 'Edward Everett Hale was the incarnation of this spirit of Boston during the 19th century.' – 'In literature he had all his culture at his finger tips.' Rev. DeNormandie mentioned an incident told him by Dr. Hale. The latter wanted to open a bank account with a first deposit of only forty-five cents. 'Upon the refusal of the bank to open an account Dr. Hale remarked: 'But you must make an exception in this case, for this sum of money represents the net profits on one of my best books.' Dr. DeNormandie called him the leading philanthropist of the century. (Forbes and Eastman, 37, 39)

GARDEN OF REMEMBRANCE 9/11

Arlington and Boylston Streets
Victor Walker, Sculptor
Stone / Granite

In honor of those who have fallen.
Taken from the Stone

Since they first disembarked from
their ship *The Arbella*, Bostonians have honored the memory of Americans who gave their
lives defending our Freedom -- from the city of
Boston or from our state of Massachusetts.

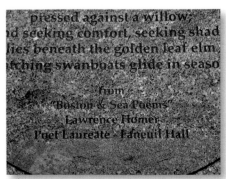

KOSCIUSZKO

Boston Public Gardens/ Boylston Street
Henry Hudson Kitson, 1927, Sculptor
Bronze / Stone

Tadeusz Andrzej Bonawentura Kosciuszko born in Poland 1746
Entrusted the Army of the United States lead by George Washington
Fought at New York and Yorktown.
A Great Patriot.
By Mrs. Henry Hudson Kitson, Sculptor 1927
Taken from the Stone

A graduate of the Military Academy in Warsaw, Tadeus Kosciuszko studied engineering in France and was a skilled military strategist. The only Polish uprising to be named after its leader is known as the Kosciuszko Uprising.

On October 18th, 1776, Kosciuszko was nominated as a colonel in the American Army. The Leader of Congress made this nomination with the words "... with great faith and trust in your patriotism, virtues and loyalty ..." On November 25th, 1783 General Kosciuszko accompanied the Commander-in-Chief George Washington on his triumphant return to New York.

The map of Colonel Kosciuszko's Revolutionary War victories include Saratoga, the turning point in the war for Independence, where "the young Polish engineer" won words of highest esteem from Horatio Gates, his commander. There is also West Point, the stronghold Washington called "the most important post in America," where Washington gave to Tadeusz Kosciuszko "chief direction and superintendence". Also at the Yadkin and Dan Rivers in North Carolina and Virginia, Kosciuszko directed the crossing and twice rescued the army from the enemy, prompting its commander, General Nathaneal Greene, to call his chief engineer "one of the most helpful and congenial companions", stressing his "perseverance, determination, indefatigable efforts" as well as his "incomparable modesty."

"From one man we can have but one life" - wrote about Kosciuszko, President Thomas Jefferson ' "and you gave us the most valuable and active part of yours, and we are now enjoying and improving its effects. Every sound American, sincere votary of freedom loves and honors you...". (www.polishworld.com/polemb/const/tk.html Jan. 21, 2011)

SUMNER

Boston Public Gardens
Thomas Ball (1819 - 1911), Sculptor
Bronze / Granite
Massachusetts State Senator 1851.

A steadfast legal guardian of Justice for all men -- in peace as well as in war. Sumner was an outspoken lawyer and orator who promoted world peace denouncing the evils of war and protested against the "slavocracy" of our Southern States.

For Championing, the cause of Emancipation, he was struck down unconscious in the Senate chamber by a Southern Congressman.
He gave the commonwealth two Washington Memorial Tablets now in Doric Hall of the State House. These are exact reproductions of the originals, which mark the graves of Lawrence and Robert Washington, the last English ancestors of George Washington.
He supported Horace Mann in his efforts to improve public education in Massachusetts.
Taken from the Stone

THOMAS CASS (1899)

Boston Public Gardens/ Boylston Street
Richard E. Brooks, Sculptor
Bronze / Stone

Another representative of Irish immigrants believing, fighting and dying for his country.

Col. Ninth Infantry USV
Fell at Malverin Hill, Virginia July 1st, 1862"
An Irish Volunteer Solider who adopted the United States as his home.
Northern Soldier without distinction of Race.
The City of Boston Replaced the Original Granite stone statue with a bronze by Richard E. Brooks 1899
Taken from the Stone

The incident of the statue of Colonel Thomas Cass, a native of Ireland, who was killed at Malverin Hill on 1 July 1863 at the head of his "Fighting Ninth" Massachusetts regiment, illustrates the Boston desire to reconcile piety and aesthetics. A granite statue of him, placed in the Public Garden in the last decade of the nineteenth century, left so much to be desired that the city replaced it by a more reputable bronze by Richard E. Brooks, at the expense of a fund bequeathed to the city by Jonathan Phillips. When the replacement was dedicated in 1899, in the presence of the subject's son and daughter, and surviving members of the regiment, Mayor Josiah Quincy (the third of his name) declared that "it represents Colonel Cass as a type of Irish soldier in the Rebellion, it is also the type of the Northern soldier without distinction of race." (Whitehill, 60)

WENDAL PHILLIPS (1811-1884)

Boston Public Gardens / Boylston Street
Daniel Chester French, Sculptor
Bronze / Granite

Prophet of Liberty. Champion of the Slave.
Whether in Chains or in Laurels Liberty knows nothing but Victories.
Made Powerful Speeches Against Slavery and For Prohibition, Woman Suffrage and Various Penal Reforms.
Dedicated July 4, 1915
Taken from the Stone

Following in the footsteps of great Boston orators, such as Daniel Webster of an earlier generation, Wendal Phillips thunders from his bronze lectern in Boston Public Gardens.

When Thomas Ball came back to Boston in 1879, the abolitionist orator Wendell Phillips (1811-1884) expressed the hope that he 'would go to heaven soon' and sent him away, as Ball recalled in his autobiography, 'with his exceedingly vulgar tirade against me and the Boston statues ringing in my ears, -as if I had made them all!' Ball's pupil, Martin Milmore, had done a bronze bust of Wendell Phillips in 1869, subsequently in 1903 presented to Faneuil Hall by the clothier A. Shuman, but neither Ball nor any one else risked attempting a statue of the sharp-tongued orator in his lifetime. Nevertheless the City Council in 1913 appropriated $20,000 for such a monument, which was executed, without fear of abuse, by Daniel Chester French. Placed in the Public Garden on the Boylston Street Mall, it was dedicated on 4 July 1915. (Whitehill, 65)

The Phillips is an intense composition. The figure has just finished pounding the lectern with his right hand while gripping links of chain in his left. This activity is controlled by a successful realization of the vertical shaft first employed by French and Bacon at Lincoln, Nebraska. In Phillips, the marble, with its sloping terminus, is unimpeded by the abundant lettering. A comparison of the two statues indicates the sculptor's preference: the relaxed, contemplative pose of the Lincoln surpasses the fiery gesture of the renowned abolitionist. (Richman, 12)

WILLIAM ELLERY CHANNING

Boston Public Gardens / Arlington Street / Boylston Street
Herbert Adams (1858 - 1945), Sculptor
Bronze / Stone

Influencing educators, politicians, philosophers and poets, a true Bostonian spiritual leader, of the 1880s, William Ellery Channing is remembered in this bronze statue.

(1780 -1842) "He preached with Spiritual Power and led a great advance toward Christian ideals." - Minister Plack of Arlington Street Church

His preaching on the abolition of slavery, civil rights for African Americans, women's rights, educational reforms and peace issues, inspired most of the important social reforms of 19th Century Boston. Dorothea Dix, the crusader for the care of the mentally ill; Horace Mann, the pioneer of the public school system; Samuel L. Gridley Howe, champion of the progressive care and education of the disabled; and Julia Ward Howe, author of "Battle Hymn of the Republic" were all his parishioners; philosophers Henry David Thoreau and Ralph Waldo Emerson were close friends and associates.

Taken from the Stone

Three Boston clergymen became statues in the early years of the twentieth century. John Foster bequeathed $30,000 for a statue of the Reverend William Ellery Channing (1780- 1842), the much beloved Unitarian divine who was minister of the Federal Street Church in Boston from 1803 until his death. With the rapid growth of the city in the second quarter of the nineteenth century, Federal Street ceased to be a residential district. Channing's congregation migrated to the new Back Bay and Boylston Street. The bronze statue of Channing that Herbert Adams (1858-1945) modeled in 1902 was, in accordance with Foster's will, placed directly opposite the Arlington Street Church, and was dedicated on 1 June 1903. (Whitehill, 75)

Esplanade / Hatch Shell Area
BRONZES & STONES

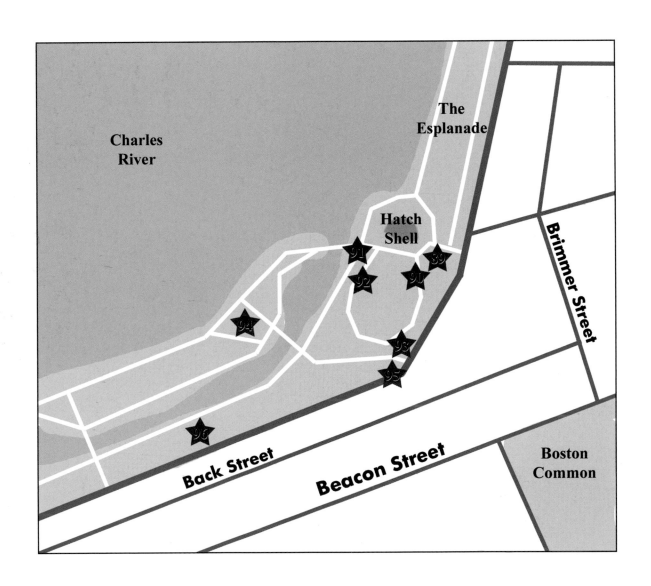

GEORGE S. PATTON

Esplanade
James Earl Fraser (1885-1945), Sculptor
Bronze

Majestically standing, George Smith Patton, Jr., a resident of Hamilton, Massachusetts and a distinguished and courageous soldier, is one of the many pillars of the WWII American Military on the Boston Esplanade.

On the Esplanade near the statues of Senator Walsh and the transplanted Civil War general, Charles Devens, stands the bronze statue of a more recent and infinitely more vivid figure, the dashing and profane General George Smith Patton, Jr. (1885-1945), the most dramatic officer on his rank in World War II. It is the work of James Earle Fraser (1876-1953), a pupil

of Augustus Saint-Gaudens, whose buffalo nickel is familiar to every American. Fraser, who also modeled the 'End of the Trail' for the Panama-Pacific Exposition, as well as sculptures for the Supreme Court and the National Archives buildings in Washington, did the statue of General Patton for the U.S. Military Academy at West Point. The Boston statue is a replica, commissioned

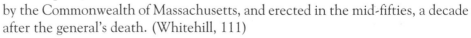

by the Commonwealth of Massachusetts, and erected in the mid-fifties, a decade after the general's death. (Whitehill, 111)

CHARLES DEVENS

Esplanade
Olin L. Warner (1844 -1896), Sculptor
Bronze / Stone

Charles Devens enlisted voluntarily into the Army of the North and proudly lead his men to victory in the southern battle fields.

Charles Devens, who has been described as "a citizen soldier and a soldier gentleman," was attending court in Worcester when it was announced that Fort Sumter had been fired upon. "You must take this brief," he said, "I must go to the armory," and with these words this first citizen of the state at that tie joined the army, rising to the rank of Major General. His record both in the war and in his many official capacities before and after is a distinguished [sic] one. He was wounded at Ball's Bluff and at Fair Oaks was promoted for gallantry, serving also at Fredericksburg and Chancellorsville. At Cold Harbor, after being wounded a second time, he was carried in a litter [sic] up and down the lines of his men, urging them on. His division was the first to occupy the Confederate Capital of Richmond, of which he then became the First Military Governor, later being made Commandant at Charlestown.

Before the war he was elected to the State Senate and served as U.S. Marshal. After the war he returned to practice law in the State, later occupying the position of U.S. Attorney-General from 1877 to 1881. He also served as Justice of the Supreme Judicial Court of Massachusetts for the five years previous to 1877 and also, from 1881 to the year of his death in 1891. (Forbes and Eastman 23)

In 1917 the New England army camp near Ayer, Massachusetts was named in his honor. The creation of a State House parking lot in 1950 caused the banishment of General Devens's statue to the Charles River Esplanade at the foot of Beacon Hill. (Whitehill, 56)

MAURICE J. TOBIN

Esplanade
Emilius R. Ciampa, Sculptor
Bronze / Stone

The political courage of Maurice J. Tobin is honored with this statue.

Tobin was governor of Massachusetts from 1946 to 1947; in 1948 he became Secretary of Labor under President Truman. In the 1938 election, in what Curley forces termed unprecedented treachery, Tobin ran against and defeated his political mentor, winning the mayor's office and serving until 1944, between Curley's last two terms.

Tobin (1901-1953) was a protégé of the legendary mayor of Boston, James Michael Curley. The Mystic River Bridge now bears his name.

Emilius R. Ciampa (1896-1996) came to Boston from Taurasi, Italy at the age of ten, studied at North Bennett Street Industrial School and briefly at Massachusetts Normal Art School. He served in France in World War I and later was in charge of art projects for Northern Art Stone Corp. of New York. Living and teaching in Medford, Massachusetts after 1928, he executed a number of memorials and bas-relief portraits.

GOVERNOR MICHAEL S. DUKAKIS

Esplanade
Granite

Michael Stanley Dukakis, born November 3, 1933, served as the 65th and 67th Governor of Massachusetts from 1975–1979 and from 1983–1991, and was the Democratic presidential nominee in 1988. He was born to Greek immigrants in Brookline, Massachusetts, also the birthplace of John F. Kennedy, and was the longest serving governor in Massachusetts history. He was the second Greek-American governor in U.S. history after Spiro Agnew.

DAVID IGNATIUS WALSH

Esplanade
Joseph A. Coletti (1898-1973), Sculptor
Bronze / Stone

A supporter of Women's Suffrage, opposed to the death penalty, and ardently opposed to the Ku Klux Klan, David Ignatius Walsh was an isolationist and believed in an independent Judiciary. Walsh was a Massachusetts Democratic Catholic leader.

David Ignatius Walsh (1872-1947), a lawyer who entered Democratic politics in his twenties, was Lieutenant Governor of Massachusetts, 1913-14, Governor 1914-16, and was elected United States Senator in 1919. Although defeated for re-election at the end of his first term, he returned to the Senate in 1926 and remained there for more than twenty years. When the Metropolitan District Commission held an open competition for a statue of Senator Walsh, the commission was awarded in 1954 to the Boston sculptor Joseph A. Coletti (born 1898). The monument, which stands on the Esplanade by the Charles River, at the foot of Beacon Hill, depicts in bronze the Senator standing against a curving wall, recalling the shape of the nearby music shell. On the wall above the statue is inscribed: NON SIBI SED PATRIAE. (Whitehill, 107)

"Not for yourself, but for the country." (Translation by Louis Jordan.)

ARTHUR FIEDLER, 1984

Esplanade
Ralph Helmick (1952 -), Sculptor
Aluminum / Granite h. 6' 4"

During my senior year in high school, I first saw Arthur Fiedler, energetically conducting The Boston Symphony Orchestra. Sitting in the first level balcony I watched his demanding intensity leading his musicians. The sculptor, Helmick depicts Fiedler's forceful musical passion in granite and layers of aluminum, an exception to our theme of bronze and stone but Fiedler was an exception in symphonic conductors.

Famed and beloved conductor of the Boston Pops Orchestra for fifty years, 1929-1979, Arthur Fiedler founded the free Esplanade concerts still performed in Boston's summer evenings at the nearby Hatch Shell.

Cambridge sculptor Ralph Helmick earned a B.A. from the University of Michigan in 1974 and an M.F.A. from the Boston Museum School in 1980. This monumental head is built up of cut out layers of aluminum in varying thicknesses, a distinctive technique originated by Helmick.

ARTHUR FIEDLER BRIDGE

Esplanade
Bronze

ARTHUR FIEDLER
BRIDGE

ERECTED IN 1953, THE 25th YEAR OF
THE ESPLANADE CONCERTS — NAMED IN
HONOR OF THEIR CREATOR AND CONDUCTOR
DEVOTING HIS MUSICAL GIFT TO THE SERVICE
OF THE PUBLIC IN HIS NATIVE COMMUNITY.
HE HAS HERE BROUGHT MUSIC OF THE MASTERS TO
COUNTLESS THOUSANDS IN THESE CONCERTS THE FIRST
TO BE PLAYED EACH SUMMER BY A MAJOR SYMPHONY
ORCHESTRA FREE TO ALL.

JAMES JACKSON STORROW

Esplanade/Charles River Park
Bronze / Stone

Best-known from the Boston highway that bears his name, James Jackson Storrow II (1864–1926) was a Boston-area investment banker who was instrumental in forming General Motors. Storrow served on the Boston City Council, 1915-1918 and was a business partner of Henry Lee Higginson, who founded the Boston Symphony Orchestra.

In 1901, Storrow initiated an effort to dam the Charles River and create the Charles River Basin, and to preserve and improve the riverbanks as a public park. The dam was approved by the legislature in 1903, and completed in 1910. The basin also eliminated tidal harbor pollution and the basin's low-tide odors.

Ironically, what the Storrows fought against, namely a highway along the beautiful Charles River, was actually constructed and dedicated in their name with this Bronze & Stone.

James Storrow had been instrumental in earlier projects along the Charles River, in particular the Charles River Dam. Additions to the Esplanade had been made during the 1930s only by omitting an important part of the project, a proposed highway from the Longfellow Bridge to the Cottage Farm (Boston University) Bridge, which had provoked tremendous protest. After Helen Storrow, wife of the now deceased James Storrow, supported a group opposed to the highway, it was dropped; part of the funding was to have come from a million-dollar gift from her. Soon after Helen Storrow's death in 1944, a new proposal for the construction of the highway was pushed through the Massachusetts Legislature. In spite of still strong opposition, and through some dubious parliamentary procedures, the bill approving construction of the highway (Storrow Drive) and naming it after James Storrow, was passed in 1949.

Fenway
BRONZES & STONES

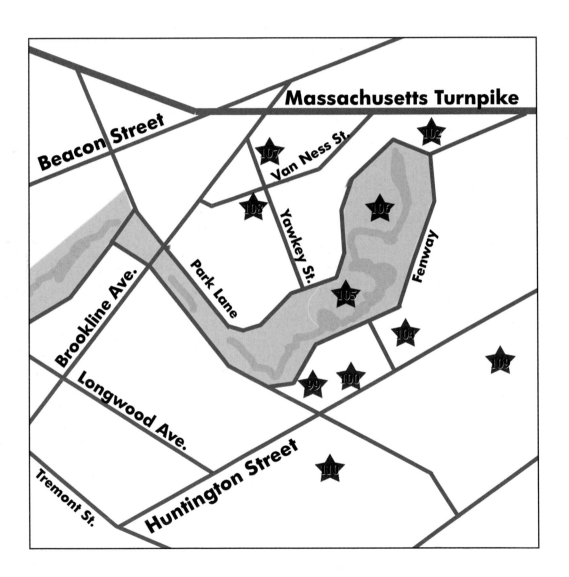

BABY HEAD

Fenway / Museum of Fine Arts / Fenway Entrance
Antonio Lopez Garcia, Sculptor
Bronze

By reopening the historic entrance, the MFA enhanced its connection to the Fenway and Longwood neighborhoods, and enlivened its relationship with the Back Bay Fens, renewing the appeal of one of the great urban parks in the country—Frederick Law Olmsted's Emerald Necklace.

The new exterior bronze, Baby Head standing 8 ft. tall and weighing 1.6 tons, compliments the new interior of MFA's Wing of the Americas.

"Antonio López García is considered a national treasure in his native Spain. We are proud to bring the extraordinary works of this contemporary realist and visionary to American audiences," said Malcolm Rogers, Ann and Graham Gund Director of the Museum of Fine Arts, Boston.

Born in 1936 in Tomelloso (part of the La Mancha area of central Spain), López displayed innate artistic talent as a youth and gained admittance to the San Fernando School of Fine Arts in Madrid at the age of 13. In the years after graduation in 1955, López was first associated with "magic realism" and juxtaposed peculiar combinations of images of people and places, resulting in mysterious and haunting compositions. Yet, by the early 1960s, the artist developed what would be his mature, realist period through which he observed his surroundings with increasing intensity and meticulously translated his view into poetic canvases, drawings, and sculpture. He has received international acclaim throughout the years, and in 2006 was awarded the Premio Velázquez (Velázquez Prize for Fine Arts), named after the 17th-century painter.

"The hallmark of López's work is its timelessness; he is an old master in the contemporary world," said exhibition curator Cheryl Brutvan (the MFA's Robert L. Beal, Enid L., and Bruce A. Beal Curator of Contemporary Art and Head of the Department of Contemporary Art). The artist is uncompromising in his truthfulness to his subjects and develops an intense relationship with each of them. His extraordinary patience allows him to create an authentic art, filled with reverence toward such humble themes.

APPEAL TO THE GREAT SPIRIT 1909

Fenway / Museum of Fine Arts / Huntington St.
Cyrus Edwin Dallin, Sculptor
Bronze / Stone

This emotional, perhaps sentimental, work won a gold medal for Cyrus Edwin Dallin at the 1909 Paris Salon. Dallin (November 22, 1861–November 14, 1944) was an American sculptor and Olympic archer.

He created more than 260 works, including well-known statues of Paul Revere and of Native Americans. He also sculpted the statue of the Angel Moroni atop the Salt Lake City Temple, which has become a symbol for The Church of Jesus Christ of Latter-day Saints, and is generally the pattern for future Angel Moroni statues on the spires of subsequent LDS Temples.

Dallin, the son of Thomas and Jane (Hamer) Dallin, was born in Springville, Utah, to a family then belonging to The Church of Jesus Christ of Latter-day Saints. At age 19, he moved to Boston to study sculpture with T. H. Bartlett, and in 1883 entered a competition for an equestrian statue of Paul Revere. No entries were selected, but over the next 58 years Dallin made seven versions of Paul Revere.

Dallin was not a member of The Church of Jesus Christ of Latter-day Saints and turned down the initial offer to sculpt the Angel Moroni for the top of the LDS Salt Lake City Temple. Dallin later accepted the job and after finishing the statue said, "My angel Moroni brought me nearer to God than anything I ever did."

In Boston, he became a colleague of Augustus St. Gaudens and a close friend of John Singer Sargent. He married Vittoria Colonna Murray in 1891, moved to Arlington, Massachusetts in 1900, where he lived for the rest of his life, and there raised three children. He was a member of the faculty of Massachusetts Normal Art School, since re-named Massachusetts College of Art and Design, from 1899 to 1941.

Dallin's works include:

- The Paul Revere statue in Boston.
- Bust of Eli Whitney in Augusta, Georgia.
- Busts of the founders of the Latter Day Saint movement, Utah's pioneers, and the Angel Moroni atop the Salt Lake City Temple.
- Monumental casts of the well-known *Appeal to the Great Spirit* outside the Boston Museum of Fine Arts in Munice, Indiana, Tulsa, Oklahoma and miniature casts that circulate and have sold at auction for up to $10,000.
- Various war memorials and statues of statesmen, generals, and mythical figures.
- More than 30 examples of his work are on display at the Springville Museum of Art in Springville, Utah.

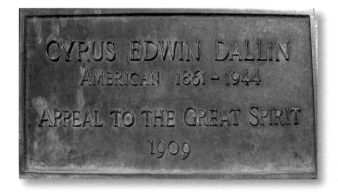

JOHN BOYLE O'REILLY

Fenway
Daniel Chester French, Sculptor
Bronze / Stone

O'Reilly proclaimed his Irish nationalist views through his prolific writing, his lecture tours, and his work in *The Pilot*. His views were well received by Boston's large Irish-born population, and *The Pilot*'s readership grew until it was one of the most read newspapers in the country. O'Reilly soon became its editor, and eventually became part-owner. Symbolizing John Boyle O'Reilly's personal traits of courage and poetic wit with Erin's two bronze sons, Courage and Poetry. Daniel Chester French captured Boyle's greatness for the Irish American people.

The moving quality of Daniel Chester French's great allegorical relief, Death Staying the Hand of the Young Sculptor, exhibited at the Paris Salon in 1892 and created for the grave of Martin Milmore in Forest Hills Cemetery in Boston, soon caused French to receive the commission for the memorial then being proposed in Boston by public subscription to another native of Ireland, John Boyle O'Reilly (1844-1890), poet, patriot, naturalized Bostonian, and editor of The Pilot. For this monument, Daniel Chester French created a double design. On one face is a bronze bust of O'Reilly set against stone background of Celtic interlaces; on the other is a bronze personification of Erin, supported by allegorical figures representing her sons, Courage and Poetry. (Whitehill, 67)

French was a modeler, not a carver. Most often he modeled in a water-soluble clay. Later in his career he would work with plasteline, an oil-based clay. (On rare occasions he executed small studies in wax). The production of the plaster that replaced the perishable clay followed immediately.

In an undated note French clarified his concern:

If the best masters in the art elaborated details . . . why may not we? Be sure that your statue is grand and beautiful and imposing enough and you may (if you are knowing enough) heighten its effect by attending to the details. If a sculptor has genius enough to create anything really great the chances are that he will have the ability to enhance its beauty by the proper amount and distribution of detail. (Richman, 23,25)

JOHN ENDECOTT

Fenway / Forsythe Way
C.P. Jennewein, Sculptor
Stone

A stern and religious Puritan, who sentenced Mary Dyer to the gallows on the Boston Common in 1660. One of Boston's earliest leaders.

In only one instance has a Boston family spent its own money to place an ancestor on a pedestal beside a public highway. This occurred in 1937 when a rather formidable stone statue of Governor John Endecott (1589-1665) by C.P. Jennewein was installed in Forsythe Way, near the Museum of Fine Arts. Funds for this memorial were bequeathed by the subject's descendant, George Augustus Peabody (1831-1929). The project was carried out by Peabody's nephew, William Crowninshield Endecott (1860-1936), who himself spared no pains to honor his stern and irascible Puritan ancestor. He had a medal by Laura Gardin Fraser struck in gold and bronze to commemorate Governor Endecott during the Massachusetts Bay Tercentenary of 1930 and persuaded Lawrence Shaw Mayo to write a biography of him, published in 1936. (Whitehill, 103)

WORLD WAR II MEMORIAL

Fenway
John Paramino (1889-1956), Sculptor / Tito Cascieri, Landscape Architect
Bronze / Stone

Boston, always the leader, built this WWII Monument before our now iconic National WWII memorial in Washington, D.C. This granite ellipse with a winged victory commemorates Boston's World War II dead.

Boston native John Paramino attended North Bennett Street Industrial School; later he was a pupil of Bela Pratt and assisted both Pratt and Saint-Gaudens. Beginning as a designer of commemorative medals and plaques, Paramino cornered the market on plaque production in Boston under Mayor Curley. In 1931 he was accused by a city councilor of running a monopoly and of charging twice the going rate, but his supporters defended him successfully. Many of the city's bronze historical markers are signed with his name. *Declaration of Independence Monument, The Lafayette Mall Monument, The Commodore John Barry Monument, The Founders Memorial, The Second Church Plaque* just to mention a few of his works.

ROBERTO CLEMENTE

Fenway
Anthony Forgone, Sculptor 1976
Bronze / Stone

Heroically, represented in bronze and stone the Boston Puerto Rican community honors Roberto with this monument and baseball field.

"Roberto Clemente: His three loves; Puerto Rico, baseball, and children".
Taken from the Stone

This monument was dedicated in 1973 to the late baseball player and humanitarian Roberto Clemente. It is a 5-foot-tall (1.5 m.) stone marker inset with a large bronze relief of Clemente and a short inscription in Spanish & English. The adjacent baseball diamond, which is part of the athletic field, is also dedicated in his honor.

Clemente played his entire 18-year baseball career with the Pirates (1955-72). He was awarded the National League's Most Valuable Player Award in 1966. During his career, Clemente was selected to participate in the league's All Star Game on twelve occasions. He won twelve Gold Glove Awards and led the league in batting average in four different seasons.

He was involved in charity work in Puerto Rico and other Latin American countries, often delivering baseball equipment and food to them.

He died in an aviation accident on December 31, 1972, while en route to deliver aid to earthquake victims in Nicaragua. His body was never recovered. He was elected to the Hall of Fame posthumously in 1973, thus becoming the first Latin American to be selected and the only current Hall of Famer for whom the mandatory five year waiting period has been instituted in 1954. Clemente is also the first Hispanic player to win a World Series as a starter (1960), win a league MVP award (1966) and win a World Series MVP award (1971).

TED WILLIAMS

Yawkey Way /Van Ness Street / Fenway
Franc Talarico, Sculptor
Bronze

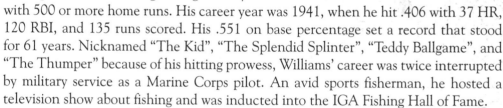

Williams was a two-time American League Most Valuable Player (MVP) winner, led the league in batting six times, and also was a Triple Crown winner. A nineteen-time All Star, he had a career batting average of .344, with 521 home runs and was inducted into the Baseball Hall of Fame in 1966.

Theodore Samuel Williams (August 30,1918 – July 5, 2002), was an American professional baseball player and manager. He played his entire 21-year career as the left fielder for the Boston Red Sox (1939-1942 and 1946-1960).

Williams was the last player in Major League Baseball to bat over .400 in a single season (.406 in 1941). Williams holds the highest career batting average of anyone with 500 or more home runs. His career year was 1941, when he hit .406 with 37 HR, 120 RBI, and 135 runs scored. His .551 on base percentage set a record that stood for 61 years. Nicknamed "The Kid", "The Splendid Splinter", "Teddy Ballgame", and "The Thumper" because of his hitting prowess, Williams' career was twice interrupted by military service as a Marine Corps pilot. An avid sports fisherman, he hosted a television show about fishing and was inducted into the IGA Fishing Hall of Fame.

Ted Williams was one of the greatest hitters who ever lived, an American patriot, and a pioneer in the development of the Jimmy Fund. Ted will forever be one of the great heroes in the history of baseball, Boston, and America. He amassed 521 home runs despite sacrificing five years in his prime to serve his country during World War II and the Korean War. He was a relentless champion of children, such as this child to whom he is offering his cap, in their battles against cancer, and helped make the Jimmy Fund at the Dana Farber Cancer Center Institute the world renowned center of research it is today.

The memory of Ted Williams will forever be a point of pride for the Boston Red Sox, the people of Boston, New England, and the United States of America.
Dedicated this 16th day of April, 2004.
Taken from the Bronze

TEAMMATES

Yawkey Way / Van Ness Street / Fenway
Antonio Tobias Mendez, Sculptor
Bronze / Stone

The Red Sox fans the world over, they are simply known as Bobby, Ted, Dom and Johnny.
Taken from the Bronze

These are our Red Sox Hall of Famers. Williams, Pesky, Doerr and DiMaggio have a permanent home at Fenway Park. Watching Ted Williams on TV hit home runs out of Fenway Park was a Sunday ritual for me and my father.

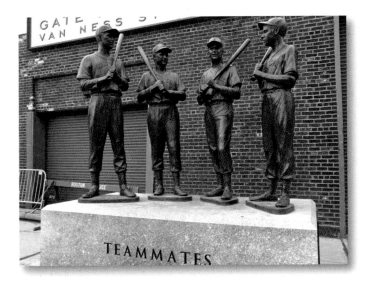

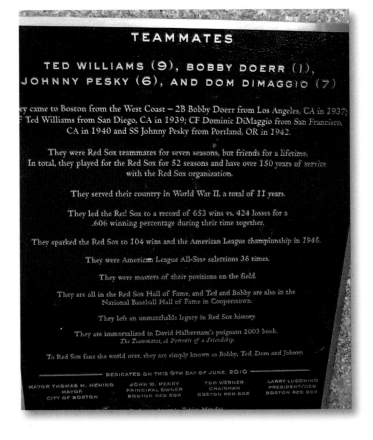

CY YOUNG

Northeastern University / Fenway
Robert Shure, Sculptor
Bronze

Cy Young, legendary pitcher for the Boston Americans (later renamed the Red Sox) came home to Boston on September 29, 1993, thanks to the generosity and commitment of the Yawkey Foundation II.

Memorialized in a bronze statue that stands on the site of the Red Sox first home field -- the Huntington Avenue Baseball Grounds, now at the heart of the Northeastern University campus -- Cy is poised in the pitcher's stance, eyes riverted on the catcher, waiting for the first pitch in the first World Series, on October 1, 1903. Although the Boston Americans lost the first game, they went on to win the series, defeating the Pittsburgh Nationals (Pirates), five games to three. In addition to the statue of Cy Young, a commemorative home plate was placed at the historic site of the first World Series. The statue, created by nationally known sculptor Robert Shure of Woburn, Massachusetts, and home plate

are located between Churchill Hall and the Cabot Physical Education Center.

This tribute to baseball and the Red Sox represents a visible link between Northeastern University and the city of Boston, a connection characterized by both changing landscapes and lasting achievements.

The Skylight Studios in Woburn, MA., the only one of its kind in New England, has performed numerous creative and historical tasks for clients in all parts of the world. Robert Shure, of Skylight Studios, also has restored many famous Boston monuments. To mention a few, the Old State House Lion and clock as well as The Massachusetts State Seal. Robert Shure has had his creative and artistic hand in "Hear Us" - State House Women's Leadership Project, The Irish Famine Memorial, The Police and Fire Memorial as well as others.

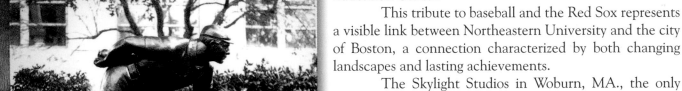

WENTWORTH LEOPARD

Wentworth Institute of Technology / Fenway
Robert Shure, Sculptor
Bronze

Crouching, *The Leopard* is ready to pounce on its prey. Robert Shure has captured that moment, that instant when predator meets its mark. A symbolic leopard represents the strength and aggressiveness of The Wentworth Institute's values of strength in skillful knowledge and adventuresome business astuteness. Applying these two characteristics, a student will succeed in life and build upon these concepts for the betterment of both the alumni and the surrounding community.

The life-like patina of *The Leopard's* spotted coat jumps out at us as his tense taunt musculature livens and softens this bronze metal sculpture, symbol of The Wentworth Institute School Spirit.

Commonwealth Ave. / Mall
BRONZES & STONES

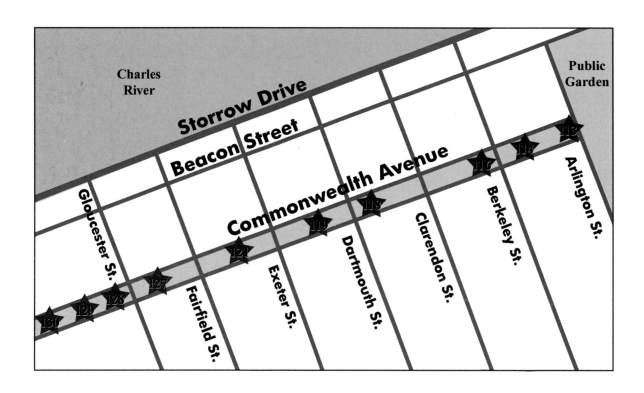

CHARLES PAGELSEN HOWARD

Commonwealth Ave / Mall /Arlington Street
Stone Bench Memorial

In Memory of Charles Pagelsen Howard (1887–1966). Lawyer, Solider, Public Servant and
Defender of the Artistic Integrity of Commonwealth Avenue
Presented to the City of Boston by the Neighborhood Association of the Back Bay and Friends.
Taken from the Stone

JOHN GLOVER

Commonwealth Ave / Mall
Martin Milmore (1844- 1883), Sculptor
Bronze / Stone

A humble fisherman from Marblehead, Massachusetts, General John Glover was a great patriot during our Revolutionary War.

H. Bowen White of Little, Brown & Company writes that he has the General's dress sword, nicely decorated. When the sword was stolen from his statue on Commonwealth Avenue this sword was used as a model to make a replacement. This statue, done in bronze, by Martin Milmore, is the gift of the city by Benjamin T. Reed. The inscription reads:
'By his courage, energy, military talents and patriotism, he secured the confidence of Washington and the gratitude of his country.'
Taken from the Stone

It is quite proper that Glover's orderly books should repose in Salem, for his ancestor Charles arrived there in 1630. The General moved to Marblehead and entered the fishing trade. Marblehead maintained a regiment and he was chosen its Colonel. In June of 1775 he and his regiment joined the Continental army at Cambridge, camping in a pasture north of the College, and later became part of the fourteenth Continental.

A scrimmage took place between these Marblehead fishermen, as they were called, and the Virginia riflemen, the latter ridiculing the former's reefer jackets and the former joking at the latter's semi-Indian costumes. It is said that Washington rushed in, and taking one in each hand, ordered them to stop wasting their strength on their friends and save it for their enemies. From Cambridge this regiment was ordered to Beverly to fit out some vessels for the navy, the "Hannah" having been the first of our navy vessels previously to be commissioned.

Glover was now generally considered as Secretary of the Navy under Washington. With his troops, Glover proceeded to New York and the battle of Long Island took place, where he and his men assisted greatly in the evacuation of the island. He later successfully helped to evacuate New York City. After long marches he and his troops fell back to Kingsbridge. He wrote:

'We fell back about three miles towards Dobbs Ferry without food or drink, and camped for the night with nothing but the earth under us and nothing but the heavens over us.'

Then followed the battle of White Plains and the crossing of the Delaware, when Glover's Regiment was called upon to man the boats, which they did with great skill. An authority stated that 'Had not John Glover's splendid regiment of seafaring men of Marblehead lent willing and skilful [sic] hands, the expedition would no doubt have failed.'

The Marbleheaders like to refer to this regiment as the "Marine Regiment," and as having given birth to the Marines, the 'soldiers of the sea.' Then came the battle of Trenton and Burgoyne's surrender; afterwards Glover and his brigade were ordered to escort the prisoners of Forge, where a grand jubilee was held on hearing of the French alliance. Again at the battle of Butts Hill on the island of Rhode Island he was obliged to superintend the ferrying of the men and supplies after a court martial upon which sat Glover; he also served as officer of the day at the time of the execution.

Glover returned home, and as his small fortune was reduced he fitted up a workshop in one of his rooms and cobbled shoes as a livelihood. From Washington's staff to the shoemaker's bench was indeed a change. He shared the sorrow of the large losses suffered by Marblehead families, for at the close of the war there were four hundred and forty-eight widows and nine hundred and sixty-eight fatherless children in the town.

Glover served as a Representative in the Massachusetts Legislature for several years and as Selectman for six years.

In 1875 Benjamin Tyler Reed gave a bronze statue of the Marblehead Revolutionary general, John Glover, to adorn the next block of the Commonwealth Avenue Mall. This was the work of Martin Milmore (1844-1883), a gifted pupil of Thomas Ball. Born in Sligo and brought from Ireland to Boston at the age of seven by his widowed mother, Milmore began when only fifteen to study with Ball. The acceptance by the city of Boston in 1867 of Martin Milmore's design for the Roxbury Soldiers Monument in Forest Hills Cemetery, when he was still in his early twenties, gave him a considerable local reputation. There a bronze soldier, resting on his gun, contemplates the graves of fallen comrades. In this work, General Glover, sword in hand, with his left foot on a cannon, seems about to spring into vigorous activity. (Forbes and Eastman 50, 5)

Alexander Hamilton

Commonwealth Ave Mall / near Arlington Street
By Dr. William Rimmer (1816 – 1879), Sculptor
Stone

Hamilton's defiant stance in this monument represents the stand he took throughout his life and against all odds. His creativity in building an American financial system enabled the United States to become a future world power.

The Gift of Thomas Lee Alexander Hamilton
Born in the Island of Nevis, West Indies 11 January 1757
Died in New York 12 July 1804
This statue erected by Thomas Lee, a citizen of Boston.
Orator, Writer, Soldier, and Jurist Financier although his
particular province was the Treasury,
his genius pervaded the whole administration of Washington.
Taken from the Stone

An orphan from the Caribbean Islands, Alexander Hamilton arrived in New York City.

When Hamilton arrived in New York, the 13 colonies had been protesting British taxes and commercial regulations for years. New York City was a hotbed of contending political factions, pitting Patriots against pro-British Loyalists. While still a student at King's College (now Columbia University), Hamilton took up the Patriots' cause, writing his first political article in 1774 (he signed himself "A Friend to America"). After war broke out, in April 1775, he joined a militia company.

He was appointed captain of the Provincial Artillery and fought in the battles of Long Island, White Plains, and Trenton.

- In 1777, Hamilton fights in the battles of Brandywine Creek, Germantown, and Princeton. He is appointed a lieutenant colonel on George Washington's staff.
- In 1778, he fights at the battle of Monmouth.
- France allies with United States.
- In 1779, Hamilton writes to John Jay, suggesting that slaves be recruited to fight, and freed.
- In 1780, he witnesses the exposure of Benedict Arnold's plot.
- Hamilton marries Elizabeth (Eliza, Betsy) Schuyler.
- In 1781, Hamilton quarrels with Washington, and resigns from Washington's staff. Later, he reconciles with Washington, and fights at Yorktown.
- In 1784, he helps found the Bank of New York.
- In 1789, Hamilton is appointed the nation's first Secretary of the Treasury.
- Washington is elected the first President.
- In 1790, Hamilton writes his "First Report on the Public Credit" and his "Report on a National Bank."
- Hamilton, in his position as first Secretary of the Treasury, took a nation that was mired in debt and gave it one of the world's first modern financial systems.
- Hamilton fights a duel with Aaron Burr, and is killed.

The filling of the Back Bay, which began in the late 1850s, and the development of Commonwealth Avenue as a local approximation of a Parisian boulevard, furnished new sites for statues. In 1865 Thomas Lee gave the city a granite figure of Alexander Hamilton that was placed in the Commonwealth Avenue Mall between Arlington and Berkeley Streets.

This was the creation of Dr. William Rimmer (1816-1879), a native of Liverpool who had been brought to Boston as a child. Although a physician with real genius as an anatomist, he eked out his living as a granite cutter, and through this sideline turned to sculpture. For the Hamilton statue Rimmer used no models, but carved directly in granite with no other guide than his knowledge of anatomy. His genius and methods were better adapted to nude rather than draped figures like this one. (Whitehill, 45)

PATRICK ANDREW COLLINS (1844- 1905)

Commonwealth Ave / Mall / Clarendon Street/ Dartmouth Street
Henry Hudson Kitson, Sculptor
Bronze / Stone

Born in Ireland and always her Lover. American by Early Training and varied employ. Upholsterer from 15 to 23.
Harvard Bachelor of Laws at 27 from 1871 Lawyer. Member of the Massachusetts Legislature 1883-89.
Member of the Congress 1893 -- 97 Consul -- General in London 1902-05.
Mayor of Boston, a talented, honest, generous man.
Placed 1908
Flanked by Mourning Figures of Columbia and Erin
Taken from the Stone

Another Irish monument, another corner stone of the Boston Irish Community.

Patrick Andrew Collins died suddenly in 1905, a meeting was called in Boston to discuss means of perpetuating his memory. In six days the funds necessary for a statue were raised, and the commission given to Henry Hudson Kitson and his wife Theo Alice Ruggles Kitson (1863-1947), who executed a bust on a high pedestal, flanked by mourning figures of Columbia and Erin. The monument was moved sixty years later to the Commonwealth Avenue Mall, between Clarendon and Dartmouth Streets.

VENDOME FIREMEN MONUMENT (1997)

Commonwealth Ave Mall Dartmouth Street
Ted Clausen and Peter White, Sculptors
Bronze / Granite

A reminder of impending death penetrates and surrounds me as I approach this work of art, this memorial for all Firemen who risk their lives for all of us each day that they stand watch.

When that Bell Rings We are All the Same,
We are a Team, We have One Job to do.
FF Thomas W. Beck with Engine Co. 32
March 22, 1937 – June 17, 1972

2:35 PM There is smoke in the Café of the Hotel Vendome on
Commonwealth Ave / Dartmouth
2:40 PM Fire Fighters arrive, finding smoke and flames
coming from the third and fourth floors
Fire Fighter Joseph F. Boucher, JRS
January 10, 1944-June 17, 1972

2:45 PM District Four Reports Box 1571 a working fire
2:46 PM A second alarm is struck
New Vendome Building in Background
Lt. Thomas J. Carroll Engine Co. 32
May 18, 1925-June 17, 1972

3:02 PM A third alarm is struck.
We save lives and property. We are no heroes.
We do what we love. We do our jobs.
- Fire Fighter Charles E. Dolan Ladder Co. 13
September 6, 1924-June 17, 1972

We don't talk about the tragic fires. It would be too much. We
go home to our families.

3:06 PM A fourth alarm is struck.
Lt. John E. Hanbury, Jr. Ladder Co. 13
May 20, 1926 - June 17, 1972

"Our families know that each day could be our last. It's just part of the work."
FF Richard B. Magee Engine Co. 33
September 17, 1932 - June 17, 1972

"The worst is death, but you learn to let go. You wouldn't be able to do your job."
5:28 PM Without warning four floors of the Vendome collapse, burying twenty-five firefighters
"There is the unknown in every fire. You do your job, follow the plan: still something can go wrong."
FF Paul Murphy Engine Co. 32
March 5, 1936 - June 17, 1972

2:00 AM Fire Fighters search the rubber until all are accounted for. Nine fire fighters are dead, sixteen are injured.
"Investigators reveal that the Vendome did not collapse because of the fire, but from structural weakness."
FF Joseph P. Sanivk Ladder Co. 13
August 8, 1924 - June 17, 1972

Sometimes you have to say
"There's nothing more we could
have done."
Losing a fire fighter brings back
every other loss."
Taken from the Stone

THE BOSTON WOMEN'S MEMORIAL 2003

Commonwealth Ave Mall
Meredith Bergman, sculptor
Bronze / Stone

THE BOSTON WOMEN'S MEMORIAL 2003: LUCY STONE(2003)

Commonwealth Ave Mall
Meredith Bergman, Sculptor
Bronze / Stone

(1818-1893) Born in Brookfield. She was one of the first Massachusetts women to graduate from college. She was an ardent Abolitionist, a renowned orator, and the founder of the women's journal, the foremost women's suffrage publication of its era.
Taken from the Stone

Lucy Stone is synonymous with Women's Suffrage. In this monument she is depicted as an intelligent, beautiful, contemplative, pondering bronze figure -- pondering the future of all women's rights.

Lucy Stone dedicated her life to writing, working, and rabble-rousing for the rights of women. Her father paid his sons' college tuition, but refused to pay his daughter's. Stone worked for nine years as a domestic laborer and teacher to earn her college tuition, and attended Oberlin -- one of very few colleges in America that admitted women at the time. After two years at Oberlin, her father, impressed by her dedication, began paying her tuition.

With Lucretia Mott, she organized the first National Women's Rights Convention, held in October 1850 in Worcester, MA. A speech delivered by Stone at the convention inspired Susan B. Anthony's decision to dedicate herself to women's rights. This speech led to the annual women's rights conventions attended by more than a thousand women and helped spark the suffragette movement.

Her husband, Henry Brown Blackwell, was a well-known activist against slavery, and both Stone and Blackwell were actively involved with the American Anti-Slavery Society. Despite their marriage, Stone retained her maiden name, and is believed to be the first American woman to do so. Stone and Blackwell founded and edited Woman's Journal, a weekly newsmagazine for the women's rights movement, published by the American Women's Suffrage Association, which Stone co-founded with Julia Ward Howe and others in 1869. She died in 1893, twenty-six years before women were granted the legal right to vote in America. (http://www.nndb.com/people/388/000160905/ Jan. 5 2011)

THE BOSTON WOMEN'S MEMORIAL 2003: ABIGAIL ADAMS

Commonwealth Ave Mall
Meredith Bergman, Sculpture
Bronze / Stone
(1744 -1818) Born In Weymouth, Massachusetts. She was the wife of the second president of the United States and the mother of the sixth. Her letters established her as a perspective social and political commentator and a strong voice for women's advancement.
Taken from the Stone

Abigail Adams lived for home and country. Her steadfast convictions guided her to do right for her husband, state, and country, as well as rights for slaves and women. Her strength, intelligence, patriotism, fidelity and mindfulness exude from this bronze by Meredith Bergman, master sculptor.

"Dissipation," was one of Abigail Adams favorite word. The time-wasting and unproductive amusements she witnessed in Paris and London were not part of Abigail's life. She was a no-nonsense leader at home, whether in Europe or in Washington D.C.. On her only voyage to London, to be reunited with John Adams after three years of separation, she lead the crew of the ship in cleaning the ship from bow to stern, and re-educated the galley on how to cook a proper meal.

Abigail Adams (1744-1818) led a life of public service and devotion to family. She was an invaluable partner to America's second president (so much so that she was called "Mrs. President"), and the educator of America's sixth president. She maintained a voluminous correspondence during her lifetime that provides a unique window into political goings-on, war, leading citizens, daily life, and her personal relationships—and her strong opinions about all. As the writer Laurie Carter Noble describes, "Her letters show her to have been a woman of keen intelligence, resourceful, competent,

self-sufficient, willful, vivacious, and opinionated—a formidable force. Her writing reveals a dedication to principle, a commitment to rights for women and for African Americans, fierce partisanship in matters of her husband's and her family's interest, and an irreverent sense of humor."

Abigail Smith was born in Weymouth, Massachusetts, to the Reverend William Smith, the pastor of the North Parish Congregational Church, and Elizabeth Quincy Smith. Both of her parents enjoyed high status in Weymouth; they instilled in Abigail a sense of duty to those who were less fortunate, and a religious life that emphasized morality and reason. Abigail often accompanied her mother on visits to the poor and the sick.

Abigail did not receive a formal education, which she always regretted with embarrassment, but she did read the books contained in her father's library and throughout her life was a voracious reader. Her intellect and spirit caught the attention of an aspiring young lawyer named John Adams in 1759. His respect for her as an equal caught her attention. By 1762, Abigail and John were exchanging flirtatious letters. In 1764, they were married by Abigail's father and moved to Braintree. Traveling from one district of Massachusetts to another to practice the law, John began to ride the circuit court and thus began the many years' worth of separation the couple would endure during their marriage. In 1765, Abigail gave birth to their first child, a daughter, named for her mother but called "Nabby."

Abigail gave birth to John Quincy Adams in 1767, and the following year the Adams family moved to Boston where John hoped to expand his law practice. The couple also became close to some of the men who were challenging Britain's taxation policies and heavy-handedness. In 1770, when outnumbered British troops fired upon an unruly mob near the State House, the soldiers were arrested and John Adams made the unpopular decision to defend them. Abigail, his most trusted confidante, supported him. The troops were found innocent, and John's career would now flourish. The family returned to Braintree briefly, but returned to Boston in 1772 where they were on hand to witness the aftermath of the "Boston Tea Party" in 1773. (http://bwht.org/adams Jan. 5 2011)

...AND BY THE WAY IN THE NEW CODE OF LAWS WHICH I SUPPOSE IT WILL BE NECESSARY FOR YOU TO MAKE I DESIRE YOU WOULD REMEMBER THE LADIES AND BE MORE GENEROUS AND FAVORABLE TO THEM THAN YOUR ANCESTORS. DO NOT PUT SUCH UNLIMITED POWER INTO THE HANDS OF THE HUSBANDS REMEMBER ALL MEN WOULD BE TYRANTS IF THEY COULD IF PARTICULAR CARE AND ATTENTION IS NOT PAID TO THE LADIES WE ARE DETERMINED TO FOMENT A REBELLION AND WILL NOT HOLD OURSELVES BOUND BY ANY LAWS IN WHICH WE HAVE NO VOICE OR REPRESENTATION.

LETTER TO JOHN ADAMS
MARCH 31, 1776

Taken from the Stone

THE BOSTON WOMEN'S MEMORIAL 2003: PHILLIS WHEATLEY

Commonwealth Ave Mall
Meredith Bergman, Sculptor
Bronze / Stone

Born in West Africa and sold as a slave from the ship "Phillis" in Colonial Boston, Phillis Wheatley (1753 - 1784) was a literary prodigy whose 1773 volume "Poem on Various Subjects, Religious and Moral" was the first book published by an African writer in America.

As a free black woman she was a mentor, breaking the old rules in order to build new ones, to inspire everyone, of any race or gender, to be more intellectually free.

She is also credited with originating the genres of African-American poetry and African-American women's literature. No one in America was willing to print her works, her first writings were published in London, England. Americans initially doubted that a slave woman could have written these poems, and so Wheatley was subjected to an interrogation by several prominent Bostonian men to determine whether she did indeed write them. They concluded that she did.

The statue is part of the Boston Women's Memorial on Commonwealth Avenue, a series of three statues of Bostonian women by Meredith Bergmann: Wheatley, Abigail Adams and Lucy Stone. This poem, which gives a taste of her work, is inscribed on the memorial:

'Imagination! Who can sing thy force?
Or who describe the swiftness of thy course?
Soaring through air to find the bright abode,
Th' empyreal palace of the thund'ring God,
We on thy pinions can surpass the wind,
And leave the rolling universe behind:
From star to star the mental optics rove,

Measure the skies, and range the realms above.
There in one view we grasp the mighty whole,
Or with new worlds amaze th' unbounded soul. '
Taken from the Stone

In July 1761, Mrs. Susanna Wheatley, the wife of a prosperous tailor with a large house on King Street, purchased a sickly eight-year-old African girl from Senegal who had been transported to Boston as a slave. By the time of her arrival, there were about 1,000 slaves in the town, whose total population was some 15,000 persons. The young girl took the name of Phillis Wheatley, and within two years she had learned English from the family with which she lived and worked. (Eminent Bostonians, O'Connor, 266)

DOMINGO F SARMIENTO (1973)

Commonwealth Ave Mall
Yvette Compagnion, an Argentine Sculptor
Bronze / Stone

Strength emanates from this monument of Domingo Sarmiento. His strength of leadership for the Argentinian people was based in Horace Mann's educational programs here in Boston, MA.

Domingo Faustino Sarmiento (February 15, 1811 – September 11, 1888) was an Argentine activist, intellectual, writer, statesman and the seventh President of Argentina. His writing spanned a wide range of genres and topics, from journalism to autobiography, to political philosophy and history. He was a member of a group of intellectuals, known as the "Generation of 1837," who had a great influence on nineteenth-century Argentina. He was particularly concerned with educational issues and was also an important influence on the region's literature.

Sarmiento grew up in a poor but politically active family that paved the way for much of his future accomplishments. Between 1843 and 1850 he was frequently in exile, and wrote in both Chile and in Argentina. His greatest literary achievement was *Facundo*, a critique of Juan Manuel de Rosas, that Sarmiento wrote while working for the newspaper *El Progreso* during his exile in Chile. The book brought him far more than just literary recognition; he expended his efforts and energy on the war against dictatorships, specifically that of Rosas, and contrasted enlightened Europe—a world where, in his eyes, democracy, social services, and intelligent thought were valued—with the barbarism of the gaucho and especially the caudillo, the ruthless strong men of nineteenth-century Argentina.

While president of Argentina from 1868 to 1874, Sarmiento championed intelligent thought—including education for children and women—and democracy for Latin America. He also took advantage of the opportunity to modernize and develop train systems, a postal system, and a comprehensive education system. He spent many years in ministerial roles on the federal and state levels where he travelled abroad and examined other education systems.

WILLIAM LLOYD GARRISON

Commonwealth Ave / Mall
Olin L. Warner, Sculptor
Bronze / Granite

My country is - the world - my countrymen are all mankind (1805 -1879)
I am in earnest - I will not equivocate - I will not excuse - I will not retreat a single inch - and I will be heard
Abolitionist - Reformer
Erected 1886
Editor of the "Liberator", Creator of the New England Ant- Slavery Society
Taken from the Stone

This William Lloyd Garrison bronze speaks to me of a brave, strong, humanist, steadfast in his moral, religious, and constitutional convictions, for all mankind.

Civil and religious, as well as military, heroes where commemorated by Boston statues during the last decades of the nineteenth century and early years of the twentieth, Some of them represented startling changes in public sentiment. In 1835 a Boston mob had dragged the abolitionist-reformer William Lloyd Garrison (1805-1879) through the streets with a rope around his neck; the rope might have been tightened had it not been for a courageous intervention

of Mayor Theodore Lyman. Half a century later a pubic subscription was being raised in Boston for a monument to Garrison. The seated bronze statue of him by Olin Levi Warner (1844-1896) was unveiled in 1886 in the Commonwealth Avenue Mall, where it keeps curious company with the likenesses of Alexander Hamilton and General John Glover. (Whitehill, 62)

SAMUEL ELIOT MORISON

Commonwealth Ave / Mall Exeter Street / Fairfield St.
Penelope Jencks, Sculptor
Bronze / Stone

Sailor - Historian (1887 - 1976)
"To my Readers young and old 'A flower sheate, a fair winde, a boune voyage'."
"Dream dreams then write them aye, but live them first."
Taken from the Stone

This stone depicts a relaxed, confident, agile sailor, seaman, and historian -- a fitting monument to a great Bostonian.

Samuel Eliot Morison used his experience as a sailor in the United States Navy to write books on the nation's naval history. He also wrote the definitive *History of U.S. Navel Operations in World War II*. Morrison wrote the 1943 Pulitzer Prize-winning, *Admiral of the Ocean Sea* and in 1959 won another Pulitzer for *John Paul Jones*. An able sailor, Morison researched Columbus' life. Born in Boston, Mass., he graduated from Harvard University and taught there for 40 years. He also wrote the popular *Oxford History of the American People* (1965) and was coauthor of the classic textbook *The Growth of the American Republic* (1930).

Other titles among his more than 50 books included, *The European Discovery of America* (Northern Voyages, 1971; *Southern Voyages*, 1974); and the 15-volume *History of United States Naval Operations in World War II* (1947-62). In addition, to the Pulitzers, he also was honored with the Balzan Prize in 1963 and the Presidential Medal of Freedom in 1964. He died in Boston on May 15, 1976.

LEIF ERIKSSON(1887)

Commonwealth Ave / Mall
Anne Whitney, Sculptor
Bronze / Stone

Historical fantasy entered the ranks of Boston statues on 29 October 1887 when a bronze figure of Leif Eriksson by Anne Whitney was unveiled in Commonwealth Avenue at Charlesgate. This was the personal whim of Eben N. Horsford, manufacturer of a patented indigestion cure called Horsford's Acid Phosphate, who by means of the statue sought to reinforce his belief that the Vinland of the Norse discoverers of America was located on the Charles River at Gerry's Landing in Cambridge. His theories were ill received, and the erection of the statue only added fat to the fire. Anne Whitney depicted Leif shading his eyes to look west into the sun setting over the Charles River. Now, alas, through recent highway construction, he peers into nothing more poetic than a vast overpass that siphons automobiles from the Fenway to the Storrow Drive. (Whitehill, 80)

The island 'No Man's Land,' owned by Joshua Crane, lying off Gay Head on Martha's Vineyard has much of interest to the antiquarians who have delved into the history of the Norsemen, for its probably served as winter quarters for all of the Vinland expeditions. Leif's house was thought by some to have been on that island. The most definite proof that on some of his voyages he landed there in the Runic inscription on a rock near the shore. Edward Gray, a former British Consul in Boston, who made a personal investigation, while preparing his book *Leif*

Eriksson, Discoverer of America A.D. 1003 studied carefully the inscription as many others have done. There were four lines of Runic lettering recording his name, with the date 1001, the last two lines, however, being undecipherable. The lettering 'Leif Eriksson – MI' was clear. The rock itself was covered except at very low water, but since the hurricane of 1938, it has slid father into the water. Gray believes that Leif may have landed near Menemsha Pond, and that his ship stranded there. (Forbes and Eastman, 25)

Copley Square
BRONZES & STONES

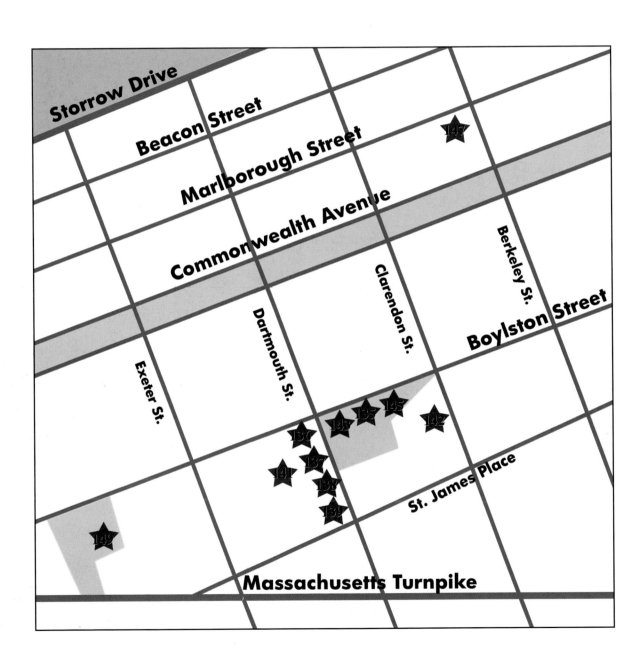

JOHN SINGLETON COPLEY (2002)

Boylston Street
Lewis Cohen, Sculptor
Bronze / Stone

(1738 - 1815) Boston and London. American Portrait Painter, Member Royal Academy of Art.
Taken from the Stone

The Copley monument honors one of Boston's greatest artists and portrait painters. John Singleton Copley (1738–1815) was an American painter, born presumably in Boston, Massachusetts the son of Richard and Mary Singleton Copley, both Irish. He is famous for his portrait paintings of important figures in colonial New England, depicting, in particular, middle-class subjects. His paintings were innovative in their tendency to show artifacts relating to these individuals' lives.

According to art historian Paul Staiti, Copley was the greatest and most influential painter in colonial America, producing about 350 works of art. With his startling likenesses of persons and things, he came to define a realist art tradition in America. His visual legacy extended throughout the nineteenth century in the American taste for the work of artists as diverse as Fitz Henry Lane and William Harnett. In Britain, while he continued to paint portraits for the élite, his great achievement was the development of contemporary history painting, which was a combination of reportage, idealism, and theatre. He was also one of the pioneers of the private exhibition, orchestrating shows and marketing prints of his own work to mass audiences that might otherwise attend exhibitions only at the Royal Academy, or who previously had not gone to exhibitions at all.

Bostonians are understandably proud of the numerous portraits of prominent Revolutionary patriots that make up a significant part of the Museum of Fine Arts. More than sixty of these portraits, including John Hancock, Sam Adams, Joseph Warren as well as Paul Revere are the works of John Singleton Copley. (O'Connor, 73)

SIR HENRY VANE

Boston Public Library / entrance / Copley Place
Frederick W. MacMonnies (1863-1937), Sculptor
Bronze / Granite

Son of an English Secretary of State, Vane the younger (1613-1662) emigrated in 1635 to Massachusetts in order to practice his strong Puritan views. A proponent of religious tolerance, he returned to England in 1637 following the Antinomian controversy that led to the banning of Anne Hutchinson from Massachusetts.

He was a leading Parliamentarian during the English Civil War, working closely with Oliver Cromwell. He played no part in the execution of King Charles I, and refused to take oaths expressing approval of the act. He served on the Council of State that functioned as the government executive during the Interregnum, but split with Cromwell over issues of governance, and removed himself from power when Cromwell dissolved Parliament in 1653. He returned to power during the short-lived Commonwealth period in 1659–1660, and was arrested under orders from King Charles II after his restoration to the throne. After long debate, Vane was exempted from the Indemnity and Oblivion Act, and was thus denied amnesty granted to most people for their roles in the Civil War and Interregnum.

Although he was formally granted clemency by Charles II, he was charged with high treason by Parliament in 1662. In a court proceeding in which he was denied counsel and the opportunity to properly prepare a defence, he was convicted by a partisan jury. Charles withdrew his earlier clemency, and Vane was beheaded on Tower Hill on 14 June 1662.

Vane was recognized by his political peers as a competent administrator and a wily and persuasive negotiator and politician. His politics was driven by a desire for religious tolerance in an era when governments were used to establish official churches and suppress dissenting views. Although his views were in a small minority, he was able to successfully build coalitions to advance his agenda. His actions were often ultimately divisive, and contributed to the downfall of the English Commonwealth. He wrote books and pamphlets on political and religious subjects that are still analyzed today, and is remembered in Massachusetts and Rhode Island as an early champion of religious freedom.

BOSTON PUBLIC LIBRARY DOORS

Inside Boston Public Library / Copley Square
Daniel Chester French, Sculptor
Bronze Relief Doors

Knowledge and Wisdom
Truth and Romance
Music and Poetry

The artistic genius of Daniel Chester French and Charles Follen McK-ims is displayed in the these Boston Public Library Bronze Relief Doors. French's participation in the Columbian Exposition had brought him into contact with Charles Follen McKim, one of the country's leading architects. During the ensuing two decades their association resulted in eight collaborations. The first was the portrait relief of Theophilus Walker (1893-94) for Bowdoin College's Walker Art Gallery. Then, between 1894 and 1902, French executed six doors for McKim's Public Library in Boston. Truth and Romance, the first pair completed, were modeled in 1897; Knowledge and Wisdom were in progress in 1898; and Music and Poetry were completed in 1902. Given the majesty of their composition and the sensitivity of the low relief modeling, the sculptor's innovative designs are excelled in nineteenth-century sculpture only by Auguste Rodin's Gates of Hell.

Commissioned by the library's architect, Charles McKim, French's door embodied a new idea in bronze door-making: instead of many narrative panels, there is one low-relief allegorical figure on each. The sculptor's daughter relates that she asked him the difference between wisdom and knowledge; French said, "Knowledge is proud that he hath learned so much – Wisdom is humble that she knows no more."

ART

Boston Public Library / Copley Place / Dartmouth Street Entrance
Bela Pratt, Sculptor
Bronze / Stone

Raphael
Titian
Rembrandt
Velasouez
Taken from the Stone

Art and Science

These lady sentinels guard the entrance of Boston Public Library's exterior, modeled and cast in bronze by Bela Pratt they were initially designed by Augustus Saint-Gaudens

SCIENCE

Boston Public Library / Copley Place
Bela Pratt, Sculptor
Bronze / Stone

Newton	Pasteur
Darwin	Cuvier
Franklin	Humholtz

Morse

Taken from the Stone

November 26, 2007–For nearly four generations, Bostonians have been welcomed to the Copley Square entrance of the Boston Public Library by two "heroic figures," as one newspaper account described them. On the left is Science and on the right, Art. They are two magnificent bronze sculptures whose creator described them as the "sisters of Literature," with literature embodied by the library itself.

Befitting a library treasure, Art and Science have a story to tell. For starters, they weren't intended to be there at all.

Augustus Saint-Gaudens, the celebrated sculptor who worked on other aspects of the Boston Public Library, had drawn up plans for the sculptures that would grace the top of the marble pedestals. A grouping of figures was to be on each. But, Saint-Gaudens died in 1907, before he could execute his plans, leaving the pedestals vacant.

One of his students, Bela L. Pratt, was chosen to succeed him on the project. As the Boston Sunday Post reported on May 15, 1910, the library's trustees had declared Pratt "the one American sculptor who could complete the work." Fittingly, he was a Bostonian (though Yale-educated).

In Pratt's hands, the sisters became finely nuanced works of art. Science holds a globe that is intended to show, as the July 20, 1912 edition of The Christian Science Monitor describes it, "the perfected whole of existence as seen through the eyes of understanding." Her eyes are downcast, her face deeply shadowed by her hood, both suggesting thoughtful repose. Art is not a mirror image, instead gazing toward Science as she holds her palette.

The same woman modeled for both sisters, Miss Ethel Nash of Brookline. For a year and a half she posed in Pratt's Harcourt Street studio four hours a day, barely moving, an hour at a time to maintain the fold and drape of the gown. The results, as one report neatly summed it up, are remarkable.

"The grand sculptures we know as 'Art' and 'Science' have welcomed millions to our palace of learning— the Boston Public Library," says Bernard A. Margolis, Boston Public Library president. (http://www.levenger.com/ AboutLevenger/PressRelease/Boston_Library.asp Jan. 21, 2011)

BACCHANTE AND INFANT FAUN

Boston Public Library
Frederick W. MacMonnies, Sculptor
Bronze

"Banned in Boston, 1896," the Boston Globe states.

This delightful light-hearted bronze piece was a gift from architect Charles Follen McKim, the designer of the original Boston Public Library. The statue depicts a nude woman holding an infant. The Boston Globe suggested that it be replaced by a "nice moral statue of a Sunday school teacher". Further comments from a local minister called it "a memorial to the worst type of harlotry with which the world was ever afflicted." McKim decided to remove it from the courtyard fountain and donate it to the New York Metropolitan Museum. The MET gladly accepted.

Several years later, George Robert White, a Boston philanthropist, obtained a second "Bacchante and Infant Faun" casting and offered it to the Boston Museum of Fine Arts which they gladly accepted as well. Boston Public Library Court Yard still has the copy and not the original gifted piece to this day. Although not an original, "Bacchante and Infant Faun" defiantly and playfully dance on the fountain's waters, meant to be an oasis for hard working academics everywhere and in every field of study.

PHILLIP BROOKS

Copley Square Trinity Church/ Boyston Street
Augustus Saint-Gaudens, Sculptor
Bronze / Tennessee Marble

Majestically, sculpted here in bronze and stone, Phillip Brooks once proudly walked the streets of Boston.

Soon after his death there was a popular demand that a statue be made to perpetuate one of America's great preachers, and a committee, composed of Martin Brimmer, President, Robert Treat Paine, Secretary, E. Winchester Donald, Edward W. Hooper, Henry L. Higginson, Col. Charles R. Codman and Alexander Cochrane was organized to receive subscriptions. The result was magical and a sum of $95,000, much more than was needed, was quickly raised. St. Gaudens was chosen as the sculptor owing to his prominence and his admiration for Phillips Brooks.

Unfortunately he died before the figure of the preacher had been begun, and the work had to be finished by his assistants in his studio at Windsor, Vermont. The completed statue was erected in 1910 on the North side of the North Transept of Trinity Church. The canopy was designed by McKim, Mead and White and is made of Tennessee marble. In 1916 the Supreme Court gave permission for another statue of the preacher, by Bela L. Pratt, to be placed in North Andover near the ancestral home of the parents of Phillips Brooks which he had inherited.

"The older generation will remember the majestic figure of Phillips Brooks as he walked the streets of Boston, a city he loved so well. In fact, on his return from Europe he is said to have exclaimed; 'There is nothing on earth so good as being a minister in the city of Boston.' And very shortly before his death, he said to one of his friends, 'What do you suppose I have been doing to-day? Why, just walking around Boston and looking at the streets and the people.' (Forbes and Eastman, 19, 21)

THE TORTOISE & THE HARE

Copley Square
Nancy Schön, Sculptor
Bronze

Tortoise and Hare, Copley Square, Boston, Mass
Bronze on brick
Height: 3"   Length 15'
Friends of Copley Square
Installed May 19,1993.

The Boston Marathon inspired the Creation of the Tortoise and Hare in Copley Square. Nancy Schön said, "I was born and grew up in Newton. The Boston Marathon has been part of my life as long as I can remember. The only marathons I haven't watched were when I lived out of state. My family had friends who lived on Commonwealth Avenue about half way up Heartbreak Hill. We would go there every year and prepare orange slices and cups of water at a little stand that we created. There were no 'official water stops' then. I loved watching the men, there were only men then, as they sweated and pulled themselves up that long, long hill - knowing that they would be able to finish the race if they could manage this tough climb. When I grew up, I became a runner, having always been an athlete. I didn't do the Boston

Marathon, just the Bonnie Belle, but I ran all year round and loved the exhilaration that it elicited.

After watching the 1991 Marathon, I started thinking about what a sculpture might be like for the Boston Marathon, the oldest foot race in the United States. I wanted to create a sculpture that would be attractive to children, yet be a meaningful metaphor for the race. I knew the marathon was based on a Greek warrior who in 490 B.C. ran approximately 25 miles to announce the news of a great military victory. The Greek connection of using another kind of race, that of the fable of the *Tortoise and the Hare* created by Aesop (?620- 560 B.C.) came to mind. I couldn't show a man running, or a woman, or a person in a wheelchair. It would be impossible to portray all the people from all over the world who run. The tortoise and the hare seemed a perfect metaphor to represent the wide variety of people who participate in the marathon - people of all ages, shapes and sizes, many of whom finish, but walk over the finish line.

Some of the marathon runners I know run just to finish, they don't expect to win, they are challenged and want to have that wonderful sense of accomplishment. Persistence pays off. Slow and steady wins the race. They want to be a part of one of the most important sports event in the country. 1996 was the 100th anniversary of the Boston Marathon. I wanted to do something to commemorate that event.

I hope that children will cherish these animals - pat them, hug them and learn the important lesson that the fable teaches. After all, children are our future and they are the runners and citizens of tomorrow."

The Friends of Copley Square have sponsored this sculpture and they believed the fable was an ideal coupling of it and the Boston Marathon. The sculpture brings a needed human factor which is significant to the neighborhood and its children.(www.schon.com/public/tortoise-hare.php Nov. 26)

BOSTON MARATHON MEMORIAL (1996)

Copley Sq. / Dartmouth St./ Boylston St.
Robert Shure and Robert Lamb, Sculptors
Mark Flannery, Designer
Bronze / Granite

The longest continuously-run annual marathon in the world, the Boston Marathon ends here with this sculpture.
Situated in Copley Square, adjacent to the finish line of the Boston Marathon, this memorial celebrates the race's 115th running. At first, the memorial might be easy to miss: instead of rising up vertically, like most of the sculptures this tour highlights, the memorial consists primarily of granite patterns set into the ground. The central medallion traces the marathon's course from the suburb of Hopkinton to Boston's Back Bay, and an elevation map shows off its notoriously difficult hills. Around this central medallion are inscribed the names of the marathon's winners, including Bobbi Gibb. Initially disguised as a man, she first ran the marathon in 1966 when women, thought to not be physiologically capable, were not yet allowed to enter the race. Depictions of the diverse runners of the Boston Marathon are captured in bronze reliefs on posts around the medallion.

Runners and Winners / Boston Marathon

JOHN WINTHROP

First Church Marlborough Street / Berkeley Street
Richard Saltonstall Greenough, Sculptor
Bronze / Stone

First Governor of Massachusetts Bay Colony at the Settlement of Boston. This bronze is a replica of the original Richard Saltonstall Greenough's marble of Winthrop that was sent to the Statuary Hall in Washington, D.C. in 1876.

Since the Commonwealth of Massachusetts had chosen as its two representatives in the Statuary Hall in the Capitol in Washington John Winthrop, Governor of the Massachusetts Bay Company at the settlement of Boston, and Samuel Adams, Revolutionary rabble-rouser and Governor of Massachusetts, 1794-1797, it was only appropriate that these worthies should be represented by replicas in Boston. Richard Saltonstall Greenough's marble Winthrop was placed in the Statuary Hall in 1876. A bronze replica of it, erected in the now vanished Scollay Square in 1880, was, because of increasing traffic, moved in 1903 to the side yard of the First Church in Marlborough Street, where memorials of the Puritan settlers of the Massachusetts Bay Company were cherished. It was seriously damaged in 1968 in a fire of unknown origin that destroyed the church. (Whitehill, 41)

Any one who has never read Governor Winthrop's diary should do so as it gives a clear conception of life here at the time of the settlement of Boston. It begins on Easter Monday, March 29th 1630, when the colonists were 'riding at the Cowes (England) – in the Arbella.' He speaks of a 'handsome gale.' The voyage was a rough one and he wrote that he would rather go to jail. Mt. Desert was sighted first and then, as the diary reads, they 'went to Mattachusetts [sic] to find a place for our sitting down.' At this same time he mentioned that they gave up toasts, 'upon consideration of the inconvenience which had grown in England by drinking one to another.'

It must have been a surprise and probably caused some concern to him and his fellow voyagers to welcome on board the Arbella, Chickatabot, who 'came with his sannups and squaws,' but his Indian visitor behaved well, and only spent one night. Later, during his many terms as Governor, Winthrop welcomed a 'dozen or so other chieftains, the most prominent of whom were Canonicus, Cutshamakin, Masconomo, Unkus and King Philip. A detailed description of these visits is given in the State Street Trust Company's brochure entitled Other Indian Events of New England.

Winthrop was extremely modest, for his diary is written in the third person, either as Mr. Winthrop or as The Governor, and at the time he took one of the Indian children, ill with smallpox, into his household, he refrains from the mention of 'I' or 'we'. In 1637 upon being reelected he wrote 'upon the election of the new governour [sic].' Old English is made use of, in an attractive way; for instance 'went' is spoken of as 'gate' and for 'sat' the expression 'sate' is used. He hardly makes mention of being chosen first Governor of the Colony shortly after arriving in 1630. He even mentions the doubtful desirability of his being reelected to the office of Governor so often, for he wrote in 1640 'Many of the elders labored much, fearing lest the long continuance of one man in the place should bring it to be for life and in time, hereditary.' In all he served eleven terms.

When Winthrop died John Cotton referred to him as having 'been unto us as a brother' – and 'as a Governor who has been unto us as a mother.' Joseph Twichell wrote that he was 'The product of the best in the generations behind, he was the prophet of the best in the generations before.' He has been described as a good mediator between the aristocratic and democratic elements, and as a prototype of Lincoln. His burial place is at King's Chapel.

Governor's Island in Boston Harbor, to be leveled and used for a fill at our great Logan International Airport, was so named because of Winthrop's ownership of it at one time. Appropriately, the old fort on the island was called Fort Winthrop. His first Boston home, incidentally, was on the site of the Main Office of the State Street Trust Company. (Forbes and Eastman 73, 74)

QUEST ETERNAL   1967

Boylston Street / Copley Square
Donald De Lue, Sculptor
Bronze / Stone

This bronze sculpture ascends upward to celebrate the construction of the then-tallest building in Boston. In 1967, the Prudential Building pioneered the future of the Boston architectural landscape. Quest Eternal proudly heralds the future for the forward-looking metropolitan business community. Lead by this tall skyscraper, our current financial district became a reality.

Found on Boylston Street in Boston, at the foot of the Prudential building - this large single cast sculpture called 'Quest Eternal' bears the following inscription: "Cast in Italy, this five-ton bronze figure is a traditional classic form depicting man reaching for the heavens."
Taken from the Stone

Park Square
BRONZES & STONES

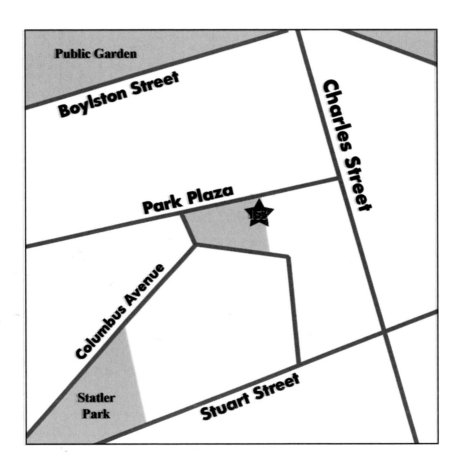

EMANCIPATION GROUP 1877

Park Square / Charles and Stuart Streets
Thomas Ball (1819-1911), Sculptor
Bronze / Stone

Freedom, release, and liberty are honored by this Thomas Ball monument.

"A duplicate casting of Thomas Ball's Emancipation Group (originally executed for the Freedman's Memorial Society in Washington) was given to the city of Boston in 1877 by Moses Kimball and put up in Park Square."(38 Whitehall).

The original version of this work stands in Lincoln Park in Washington, D.C.

The Great Emancipator freeing a male African-American slave modeled on Archer Alexander. The ex-slave is depicted crouching shirtless and shackled at the president's feet.

The monument has long been the subject of controversy. Despite being paid for by African-Americans because of the supplicant and inferior position of the black figure, historian Kirk Savage in 1997 condemned it as "a monument entrenched in, and perpetuating, racist ideology."

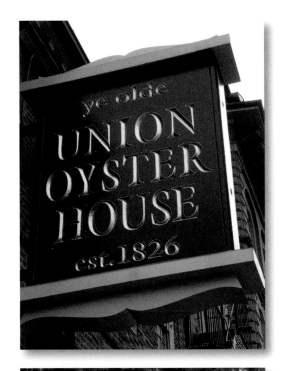

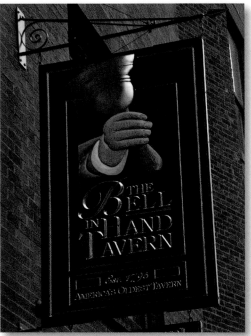

Chinatown / Theater District
BRONZES & STONES

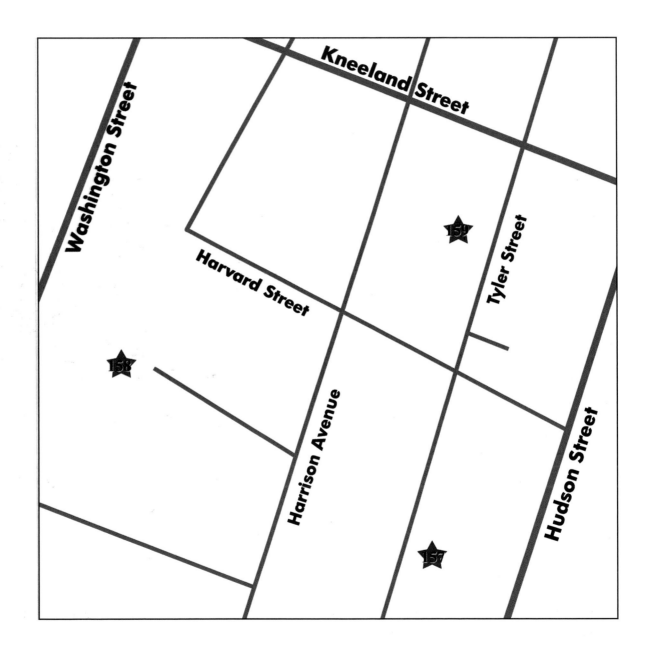

CONFUCIUS, C. 1984

Chinatown / Tyler Street
Taiwanese artist, name unknown
Sand Stone / Granite / Bronze

Confucius, China's great philosopher, is shown -- peaceful, contemplative, and always serene -- by an unknown Taiwanese artists. China's ancient wisdom and beliefs are honored in this statue -- a gift to the Chinese Consolidated Benevolent Association of Boston from the government of Taiwan -- for the people of Boston's Chinatown. One of my most elusive Boston bronze finds, "Confucius" is well-placed on a quiet corner of Chinatown away from the daily activities of this vibrant part of our city.

The philosophy of Confucius emphasized personal and governmental morality, correctness of social relationships, justice and sincerity. These values gained prominence in China over other doctrines, such as Legalism and Taoism during the Han Dynasty (206 BC – AD 220). Confucius' thoughts have been developed into a system of philosophy known as Confucianism

Because no texts survive that are demonstrably authored by Confucius, and the ideas most closely associated with him were elaborated in writings that accumulated over the period between his death and the foundation of the first Chinese empire in 221 BC, many scholars are very cautious about attributing specific assertions to Confucius himself. His teachings may be found in the *Analects of Confucius*, a collection of aphorism, which was compiled many years after his death. For nearly 2,000 years he was thought to be the editor or author of all the Five Classics such as the Classics of Rites, and the Spring and Autumn Annals.

Confucius' principles had a basis in common Chinese tradition and belief. He championed strong familial loyalty, ancestor worship, and respect for elders by their children .

TEDDY BEAR, 1991

Chinatown / Tremont Street
Robert Shure (1948 -   ), Sculptor
Bronze

Originally located at Boylston and Berkeley Streets, Teddy Bear is more at home cheering up both adult and child patients at Boston's Floating Hospital for Children. Sculptor Robert Shure became an assistant to Cascieri and di Biccari (see Boston Common: Parkman Plaza), and continues their traditional style of commissioned sculptures at his Skylight Studios in Woburn. Just some:

RECENT COMPLETED COMMISSIONS

Massachusetts Korean War Memorial - Charlestown Navy Yard
Catherine Filene Shouse Memorial - Charlestown Navy Yard (inside)
In Tribute to Boston Police Officers - Boston Police Headquarters
FAO Teddy Bear - New England Medical Center
Cy Young Memorial - On Northeastern University campus (site of 1st World Series)
Ted Williams Tunnel Plaques (at 2 entrance of Tunnel)
Donald McKay Memorial - East Boston - Bremen St Park
South Boston WWII Memorial - on beach -Day Blvd.

Freedom Trail Bronze plaques - in sidewalks - Boston
Replica sculptures & clock - Old State House)
Irish Famine - @ School & Washington Street
Women Suffrage portraits - Massachusetts State House (inside)
    (Stone, Dix, Luscomb, O'Sullivan, Ruffin, Redmond)
Numerous plaques - Massachusetts State House (inside)
E. Virginia Williams relief - Boston Ballet (inside)
Don Orione Statue - Don Orione Shrine, E. Boston
Massachusetts Fallen Firefighters Memorial - Massachusetts State House (Sept. - 2007)
Boston Fireman & Policeman Memorial - Two International Place (inside)
Clara Barton portrait - Massachusetts State House (inside)
Wentworth Leopard - Wentworth University
Bronzes at finish lane of Marathon

IN TRIBUTE TO BOSTON POLICE OFFICERS 2005

Robert Shure, Sculptor
Bronze / Stone

After a decade of planning, the Boston Police Department's legacy of more than 150 years -- the oldest police department in the USA -- was finally immortalized. Since 1854, from the first watchmen to today's Boston's Police Force, Boston Police Officers have given their lives in the line of duty. The unveiling of this memorial was completed and dedicated with Police Commissioner Kathleen M. O'Toole, Mayor Menino, 500 residents, and Rita Gallagher, 76, of South Boston. Rita's husband, John, was shot dead at 33 years of age, in the line of duty.

"This is beautiful," she later told Bob Shure of Skylight Studios in Woburn, who created the memorial. "I just had to say that to you." The idea, the planning, the fund raising and the hard work to complete this police memorial for the oldest and finest police force in the country was accomplished by Capt. Bob Flaherty commander of the 4th District of the South End. The memorial was funded by officers, civilian employees and private grants that took over 10 years and $500,000 to complete.

School Street / Old City Hall
BRONZES & STONES

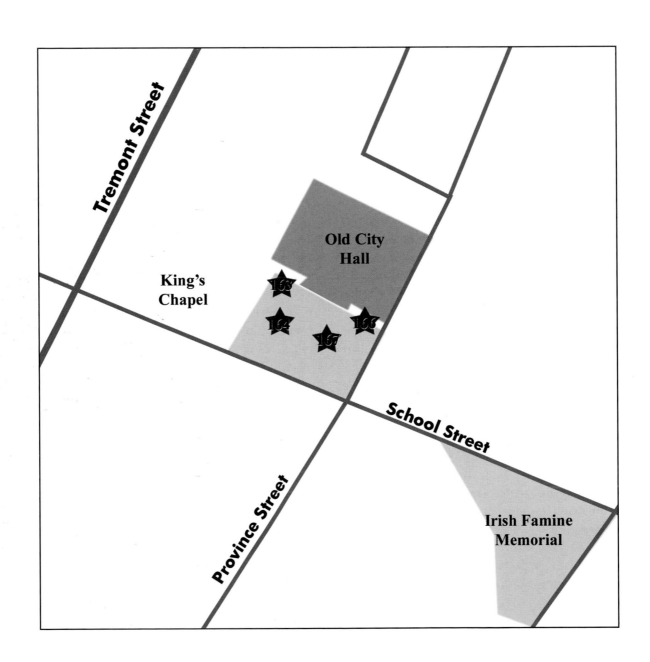

Tremont Street

King's
Chapel

Old City
Hall

163

164

165

167

School Street

Province Street

Irish Famine
Memorial

JOSIAH QUINCY

Old City Hall / School Street
Thomas Ball (1819- 1911), Sculptor
Bronze / Granite

Josiah Quincy (1772-1864) was the second Mayor of Boston and served six consecutive, one-year terms from 1823 to 1828. During his tenure he was responsible for the development that expanded the produce and meat markets in Faneuil Hall into three new buildings known as the Quincy Markets. This statue (1879) was designed by Thomas Ball. (http://www.old-cityhall.com/history.html Jan. 4, 2011)

Son of a Charlestown house and sign painter, Ball began his career as a self-taught portrait painter. It did not go well, and he found other income as a church choir soloist. Turning to portrait busts, Ball found success with images of Jenny Lind and Daniel Webster, later mass-duplicated for public sale. At age thirty-five Ball went to study sculpture in Florence, returned to Boston for eight years during which he constructed the equestrian Washington for the Public Garden and other works, then settled in Florence for the next thirty years, dean of the expatriate American artistic community.

CITY CARPET, (1983)

School Street
Lilli Ann Killen Rosenberg, Sculptor
Bronze / Stone

Boston Latin School, with its unique concept of free education (for boys only, however), was established in 1635. Boston Latin remains a prestigious public school and the oldest educational institution in the country, antedating Harvard by a year.

Shaped like a hopscotch grid, this mosaic marks the original site of the Boston Latin School, the first public school in the US. The school educated many influential politicians and writers, including Benjamin Franklin and Ralph Waldo Emerson. Although girls are depicted in the images of children at play, no girls were admitted to the school until the mid-19th century; the school became officially co-educational in 1972. Another mosaic by New England artist Lilli Ann Killen Rosenberg is located near Frog Pond in the Boston Common.

BENJAMIN FRANKLIN

Old City Hall / School Street
Richard Saltsonstall Greenough, Sculptor
Bronze / Stone

Benjamin Franklin (1706-1790), famous as a scientist, inventor, journalist, philosopher, and an ambassador of Colonial America and the young Republic, was born on Milk Street in Boston.

The bronze panels on the four sides of the plinth depict highlights from Franklin's life: as a printer; signing the Declaration of Independence; signing the Treaty of Peace with France; and experimenting with lightning and its potential for creating electricity.

It is interesting to know that the first letter to be carried by air was delivered to his household while he was in France as a representative of our government. This was particularly appropriate as Franklin had been the first Postmaster-General of the United States. By coincidence, the letter was carried by another Bostonian, Dr. John Jeffries, on the first flight by balloon across the English Channel on January 7, 1785.

A few years earlier, on December 6, 1782, in referring to experiments then going on with balloon ascensions, Franklin demonstrated his amazing imaginative powers by stating, in the following words, that aircraft might possible give a new turn to human affairs. 'Convincing sovereigns of the folly of wars may be one effect of it … since 5,000 ships of the line; and where is the prince who can afford so to cover his country with troops for its defence [sic] as that 10,000 men descending from the clouds might not in many places do an infinite deal of mischief before a force could be brought together to repel them.' And that was more than a century and a half before paratroopers did such devastating work in World War II.

One of the postal balloons sent up from Paris during the siege of 1870 was named "Le Franklin." A copy of one of the letters carried by balloon from Paris is in the Aviation Collection of the State Street Trust Company, at its Union Trust Office.

There are about thirty towns with post offices in this country named for Franklin. (Forbes and Eastman, 33)

DEMOCRAT DONKEY

Old City Hall / School Street
Antonio Frilli, sculptor / inspired by cartoonist Thomas Nast
Bronze

In 1828, Andrew Jackson established the Democratic party and ran for president using the populist slogan, "Let the people rule." His opponents thought him silly and labeled him a "jackass." Jackson, however, picked up on their name calling and turned it to his own advantage by using the donkey on his campaign posters. Over the years this donkey has become the accepted symbol of the Democratic party.

The symbol of the Republican party in 1974 was born in the imagination of a cartoonist, Thomas Nast, in Harper's Weekly. Soon other cartoonists used the elephant to symbolize Republicans, and eventually, Republicans adopted the elephant as their official symbol. (http://www.oldcityhall.com/history.html Jan. 4, 2011)

This site was the location of two Boston City Halls. Here in 1810, the Suffolk Country Courthouse was erected. In 1841, that courthouse was converted to Boston's second city hall. In 1865 it was replaced by Boston third city hall, the building you see today on School Street. In 1969, Boston built its fourth city hall at Government Center and vacated this site.

Thirty-eight Boston mayors served their terms of office on School Street at this site over a period of one hundred and twenty-eight years. All twenty of the Democratic mayors adopted the donkey as their party's symbol, while only five of the ten Republican mayors utilized the elephant.

In front of the donkey, footsteps with little elephants engraved in them "stand in opposition." These two artistic pieces cast in bronze are symbolic of the embryonic two-party political system beginning with Thomas Jefferson's Republican Party and John Adams Federalist Party which has evolved into today's system. Created by Antonio Frilli of the famous Florentine Art Gallery. Since 1860, this Italian gallery has manufactured hand-carved Cararra marble and "lost wax" bronze castings such as this one.

HISTORIC BURYING GROUNDS INITIATIVE

KING'S CHAPEL
BURYING GROUND

ESTABLISHED
1630

NATIONAL REGISTER OF
HISTORIC PLACES

VISITORS PLEASE TAKE NOTICE

No gravestone rubbing.
Do not sit or lean on tombs or gravestones.
No alcoholic beverages.
No dogs allowed.

This burying ground is a place of honor and history.
The condition of the gravestones is the result of time and the effects of weathering.
Preserve this site for future generations by treating it with respect.
This site is open during daylight hours.

Park users are subject to the rules and regulations of the Parks Commission,
City of Boston, Parks and Recreation Department: 635-4505.
In case of emergency, please call 911.

HISTORIC BURYING GROUNDS INITIATIVE

GRANARY
BURYING GROUND

ESTABLISHED
1660

NATIONAL REGISTER OF
HISTORIC PLACES
BEACON HILL ARCHITECTURAL DISTRICT

VISITORS PLEASE TAKE NOTICE

No gravestone rubbing.
Do not sit or lean on tombs or gravestones.
No alcoholic beverages.
No dogs allowed.

This burying ground is a place of honor and history.
The condition of the gravestones is the result of time and the effects of weathering.
Preserve this site for future generations by treating it with respect.
This site is open during daylight hours.

Park users are subject to the rules and regulations of the Parks Commission,
City of Boston, Parks and Recreation Department: 635-4505.
In case of emergency, please call 911.

PAUL REVERE
BURIED IN THIS GROUND

This tablet as a memorial to Paul Revere
is erected by the
Paul Revere Memorial Association to
commemorate the opening to the public
on April 19, 1908
of his old house at No. 19 North Square
in this city.
May the youth of today when they visit
this old house be inspired with the
patriotism of Paul Revere

HERE LIES BURIED
SAMUEL ADAMS
SIGNER OF THE DECLARATION OF INDEPENDENCE
GOVERNOR OF THIS COMMONWEALTH
A LEADER OF MEN AND AN ARDENT PATRIOT
BORN 1722   DIED 1803

MASSACHUSETTS
SOCIETY

SONS OF THE
REVOLUTION

1898

King's Chapel
BRONZES & STONES

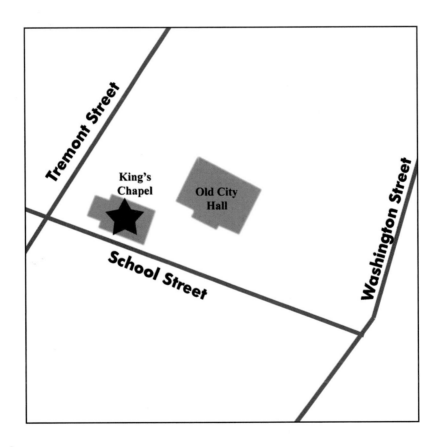

All the artwork in this section is located inside King's Chapel,
located on the corner of Tremont Street and School Street

KING'S CHAPEL

Corner of Tremont and School Street

In 1870 The Statues Hall in Washington D.C. began receiving its first statues from Boston artists. Apart from the statues of Governor Winthrop and Samuel Adams in the Capitol pantheon, what did Boston do about statues in the nineteenth century, and who was commemorated? For the first half of the century, the answer is "almost nothing," for there were no local sculptors capable of heroic statuary in bronze or marble. An eighteenth century Bostonian with an itch for memorialization was obliged to send to London. The most that any of them aspired to was a memorial tablet, with no more than a bust, by way of portrait. Three characteristic examples of this type of commemoration are still to be seen on the walls of King's Chapel, an enchanting building that still preserves the flavor of Tory-Anglican, pre-Revolutionary Boston.

It seems likely that the three memorial tablets imported from England were allotted space in King's Chapel because their donors had contributed to the construction of the present build-ing. The Church of England first came to Puritan Boston in 1686, when royal authority was definitely established there with the sending of Sir Edmund Andros as the first royal governor of the Province of Massachusetts Bay. Angli-can services were initially held in the Town House; then, to the disgust of its rightful congregation, in the Old South Church. Finally in 1689 a modest wooden King's Chapel, built in one cor-ner of the old burying ground at Trem-ont and School Streets, was opened for Anglican worship. Although enlarged in 1710, this building was by 1741 so in-adequate and in such poor repair that it was proposed that it be rebuilt of stone. To this end a subscription paper was cir-culated, on which two of the more gen-erous pledges were made by sometime

wardens of the church, William Shirley (1693-1771), Governor of the Province of Massachusetts Bay, 1741-1756, and Charles Apthorp (1698-1758), a merchant who had greatly prospered through army contracting. Although the first subscription languished, a second was undertaken in 1747, with Apthorp as treasurer. Again both he and Governor Shirley made generous pledges. (Whitehill, 8, 9)

SAMUEL VASSALL (1586-1667)

Inside / King's Chapel / School / Tremont Streets
William Tyler, Sculptor
Carrara Marble

The Samuel Vassall statue, carved by an Englishman, is one of the first stone monuments, other then gravestones, to be placed in North America.

This eighteenth-century London sculptor represented in King's Chapel is William Tyler, R.A. (died 1801), who, in 1766, carved the monument to Samuel Vassall (1586-1667) that stands on the west wall, left of the principal entrance to the church. The Boston presence of a bust of a seventeenth century member of Parliament, who never set foot in New England, is an indirect consequence of the fund-raising of the 1740s. In 1748, when local contributions dragged, appeals were broadcast to potential benefactors in England and friendly colonies. Among these was one sent to William Vassall in Jamaica, accompanied by a subscription form addressed. "To all charitable and well disposed Gentlemen in the Island of Jamaica." It did not produce any remarkable results, although Florentius Vassall, whose life was spent between Jamaica and England, did subscribe ten guineas. A dozen years after the church was in use, however, Florentius shipped to it this monument to his great-grandfather, with the request that it be erected in King's Chapel. The political views of the subject, who was described as "a steady and undaunted asserter of the Liberties of England," were opposite-minded enough to appeal to some Bostonians in 1766, for the 1628 'he was the first,' so the inscription states, 'who boldly refused to submit to the tax of Tonnage and Poundage, an unconstitutional claim of the Crown arbitrarily imposed: For which (to the ruin of his family) his goods were seized and his person imprisoned by the Star Chamber Court.' But, he had his say later, for he was elected an M.P. for London in the Short and Long Parliaments of 1640, and in due course was voted by Parliament £10445/12/2 for his damages. This fact was recorded, down to the pennies, in the lengthy inscription that William Tyler carved on the monument. It was so large that it could only be installed by removing pew 43, on the North side of the West door; as Vassall's representative in Boston paid £33/6/8 for the pew, the monument was accordingly put in its present location, where it has puzzled many church-goers and visitors ever since. (Whitehill 13, 14)

FRANCES BARKER SHIRLEY MONUMENT

Inside King's Chapel / School / Tremont Streets
Peter Scheemakers (1691-1781), Sculptor
Stone / Carrara Marble

This Frances Barker Shirley Monument is one of the first of the non-American made statues in North America. In 1749 Peter Harrison completed plans for the present stone King's Chapel. Construction was begun in 1750, although it was August 21, 1754 before it was used for service. On the wall of the south aisle, beside the royal governor's canopied box pew, William Shirley promptly placed a monument in memory of his wife, Frances Barker, who had died in 1744. This took the form of a tablet, with an immensely long Latin inscription setting forth the virtues of both ladies, surmounted by a charming bust of one of them. As befitted such a memorial offered by a man of Shirley's position, it was by the London sculptor, Peter Scheemakers (1691-1781), who had in 1740 carved the monument to Shakespeare in Westminster Abbey. The artist was a native of Antwerp, the son of a sculptor, who had walked to Copenhagen and then to Rome for study before settling in London about 1716.

There he remained, busily at work, until 1771, when, as an old man, he returned to Antwerp. Of the sixty-nine monuments by Peter Scheemakers listed by Rupert Gunnis in his Dictionary of British Sculptors, 1660-1851, fourteen are in Westminster Abbey, while busts that Scheemakers did of Milton, Spenser, Shakespeare, and Dryden were presented by Frederick, Prince of Wales, to Alexander Pope. The Shirley monument is, according to Rupert Gunnis's list, the only work by Scheemaker in British North America. (Whitehill 9)

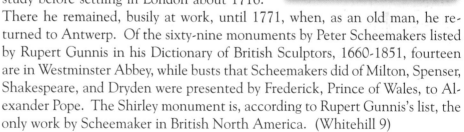

APTHROP MEMORIAL

Inside King's Chapel / School / Tremont Streets
Sir Henry Cheere (1703-1781), Sculptor
Cararra Marble

These statues represent more of the non-American made statues to be exhibited in North America.

"When Charles Apthrop died in 1758, he was elegantly commemorated in the North aisle of King's Chapel with a tablet executed by Henry Cheere (1703-1781) of London. Here too there is a sonorous Latin inscription, characterizing the deceased as surmounted, not by a portrait bust, but by a plump cherub, weeping beside an urn. As Apthrop's wife and five-sixths of their eighteen children had survived him, the inscription concludes grandiloquently" (Whitehill, 10, 11)

"On the inscription - Whitehill says the inscription concludes grandiloquently, that is in lofty, pompous, or bombastic style. Indeed this is a highly rhetorical style. Apthrop is not just an upright merchant but (using the superlative) a most upright merchant. He is not just a citizen of probitas (that is integrity, honesty or probity) but insigni (that is, remarkable, distinguished or conspicuous) probitate. (Translated by Louis Jordan)

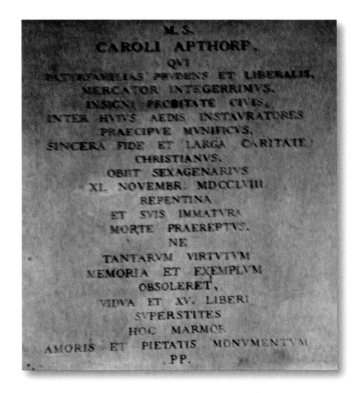

M.S. [MONUMENTUM STATUIT]	This monument was erected
CAROLI APTHORP,	For Charles Apthorp
QUI	Who was
PATERFAMILIAS PRUDENS ET LIBERALIS,	A prudent and generous patriarch,
MERCATOR INTEGERRIMUS,	A most upright merchant,
INSIGNI PROBITATE CIVIS,	A citizen of remarkable integrity,
INTER HUIUS AEDIS INSTAURATORES	Among those who had restored this sanctuary
PRAECIPUE MUNIFICUS,	Generous above others,
SINCERA FIDE ET LARGA CARITATE	With sincere faith and abundant Christian charity
CHRISTIANUS,	
OBIIT SEXAGENARIUS	He died unexpected at sixty years old
XI NOVEMBR, MDCCLVIII,	11 November 1758
REPENTIA	and by his premature death
ET SUIS IMMATURA	he has been carried off
MOTRE PRAEREPTUS	
NE	Lest the memory and example
TANTARUM VIRTUTUM	Of such virtues
MEMORIA ET EXEMPLUM	Might fade away
OBSOLERET,	
VIDUA ET XV LIBERI	You may be kept alive
SUPERSTITES	By your widow and 15 children
HOC MARMOR	And this marble
AMORIS ET PIETATIS MONUMENTUM	A monument of love and piety.
PP. [PERPETUUS]	In perpetuity

Like Governor Shirley, the Apthorps had recourse to a stylish London craftsman, for Henry Cheere had in 1733 executed the statute of Queen Caroline for Queen's College, Oxford, and in 1734 one of William II for the Bank of England. Of the twenty-nine monuments attributed to him by Rupert Gunnis, nine are in Westminster Abbey. The Apthorp memorial, his only work in British North America, was also his last of this type, for honors crowded in upon him. In 1760 he was knighted, when he presented a congratulatory address to George III from the County of Middlesex; in 1766 he was created a baronet, and in 1770 he gave up his yard near Hyde Park Corner and retired from business. (Whitehill 11,12)

SAMUEL APPLETON

King's Chapel / School Street / Tremont Street
Marble / Carrara Marble

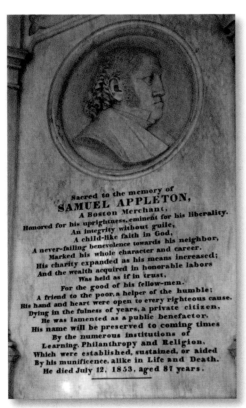

A monument to a good citizen, a good Anglican, farmer, merchant, teacher, husband, parishioner, and educational philanthropist. Appleton was born in New Ipswich, New Hampshire. From 1790 to 1792, he cleared fields in Maine for farming. He also taught school. For a time he kept a store in Ipswich. In 1794, he moved to Boston where he became an importer, in partnership with his brother Nathan, as S. & N. Appleton, buying European dry goods at auction and for resale to country traders in exchange for homespun cloth as well as pot and pearl ash for export to Britain. He also later established cotton mills at Waltham and Lowell, Massachusetts. After 1799 he passed much of his time in Britain, and at age 53 married a widow, Mrs. Mary Gore, with whom he had no children. He retired from business in 1823.

Samuel Appleton tomb is in Mount Auburn Cemetery. After retirement he devoted much of his fortune to charity, including his gift funding the Appleton Cabinet at Amherst College, built to house the Hitchcock Ichnological Cabinet, and Appleton Chapel at Harvard University. Appleton served as a vestryman of King's Chapel from 1830 to 1840, and monument to him sits on the North wall of the chapel.

Wilson's biographical directory of Boston's business aristocracy, published 1848, noted that it was "to the credit of Samuel Appleton, that he commenced life with a single four-pence half penny, paid to him by a drover who passed his father's house, for assistance in driving cattle.

Sacred to the memory of
SAMUEL APPLETON,
A Boston Merchant,
Honored for his uprightness, eminent for his liberality.
An integrity without guile,
A child-like faith in God,
A never-failing benevolence towards his neighbor,
Marked his whole character and career.
His charity expanded as his means increased;
And the wealth acquired in honorable labors
Was held as if in trust,
For the good of his fellow-men.
A friend to the poor, a helper of the humble;
His hand and heart were open to every righteous cause.
Dying in the fulness of years, a private citizen,
He was lamented as a public benefactor.
His name will be preserved to coming times
By the numerous institutions of
Learning, Philanthropy and Religion,
Which were established, sustained, or aided
By his munificence, alike in Life and Death.
He died July 12, 1853, aged 87 years.

Downtown / Financial District
BRONZES & STONES

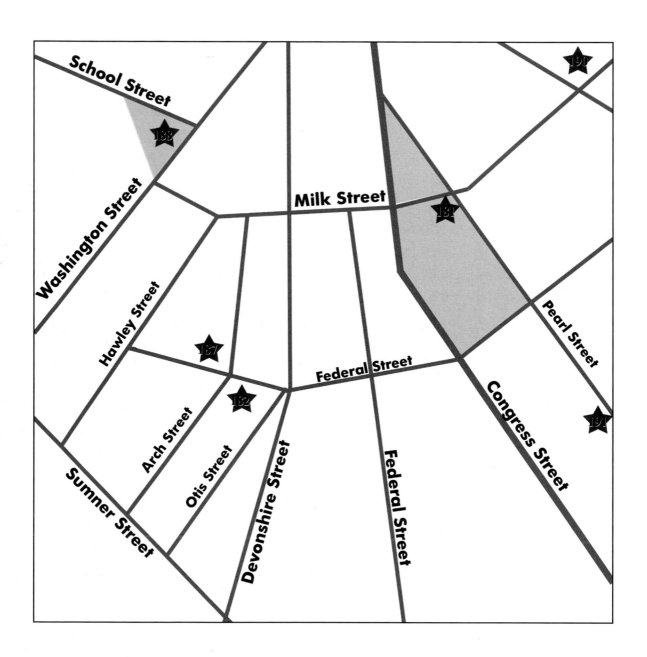

The Creature Pond, 1982

Downtown / Post Office Square
Collaboration: Lowry Burgess, Donald Burgy, John Cataldo, Carlos Dorrien, Robert Guillemin,
David Phillips, Sydney Roberts Rockefeller, William and Clara Wainwright
Bronze / Granite

Compassionate animal lover George Thorndike Angell was an American lawyer, philanthropist, and advocate for the humane treatment of animals. While attending horse races in 1866, he witnessed two horses being run to death. Motivated by this incident in New York, his advocacy for the humane treatment of animals became a lifelong passion.

In 1868 he founded and became president of the Massachusetts Society for the Prevention of Cruelty to Animals in the same year establishing and becoming editor of *Our Dumb Animals*, a journal for the promotion of organized effort in securing the humane treatment of animals. For many years he was active in the organization of humane societies in England and America. In 1882 he initiated the movement for the establishment of *Bands of Mercy* (for the promotion of humane treatment of animals), of which in 1908 there were more than 72,000 in active existence. In 1889 he founded and became president of the "American Humane Education Society".

He was also a pioneer in bringing awareness to the kindness to animals. This bronze and granite depicts animals and nature with all its tranquility. Also the site of the first post office in America, 1639.

BOSTON BRICKS

Winthrop Lane / between Otis / Arch streets
Kate Burke and Gregg Lefevre, Sculptors
Bronze / Stone

Used as pavers among the common cobblestones, "Boston Bricks" speak quietly to us about the Boston Tea Party, The Boston Marathon, and Boston's reputation for horrific drivers and traffic. Each bronze brick work of art depicts dozens of past historical events. Some of these tiny vignettes are comical and some are monumental, each cast in bronze surrounded by stone and bricks, hidden in Boston's downtown district.

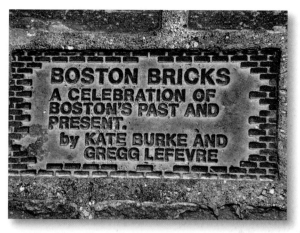

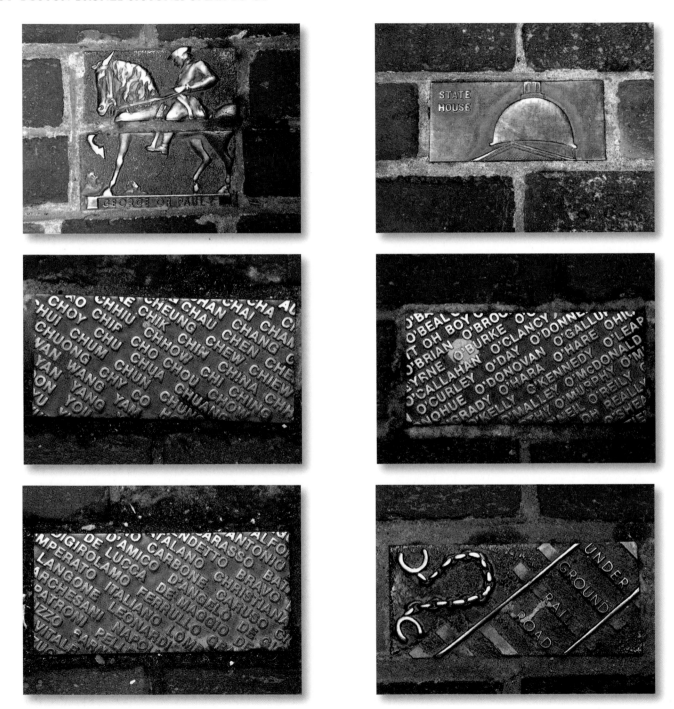

ROBERT BURNS

Downtown / Winthrop Square
Henry Hudson Kitson, Sculptor
Bronze / Granite

The Robert Burns statue, like a number of Boston statues, has been relocated to Winthrop Square in the heart of downtown Boston. The movement and candor embodied in this swashbuckling statue is befitting of Robert Burns, author of "Auld Lang Syne," and many other original compositions. Burns also collected folk songs from across Scotland, often revising or adapting them.

Homesick Scots, when they reach a certain state of solvency, can never resist putting up a statue of Robert Burns. A charming bronze figure by Henry Hudson Kitson of the poet, book in hand, accompanied by a collie dog, was presented to the city of Boston by the Burns Memorial Association. After four previous attempts to find a suitable location, it was in 1920 installed in a thicket near the Muddy River, behind the fire alarm

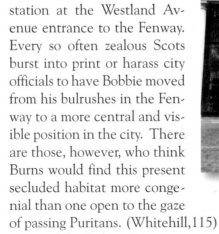

station at the Westland Avenue entrance to the Fenway. Every so often zealous Scots burst into print or harass city officials to have Bobbie moved from his bulrushes in the Fenway to a more central and visible position in the city. There are those, however, who think Burns would find this present secluded habitat more congenial than one open to the gaze of passing Puritans. (Whitehill,115)

The Robert Burns statue currently resides at One Winthrop Square.

IRISH FAMINE MEMORIAL

Downtown / Chauncey / Washington Street
Robert Shure, Sculptor
Bronze / Stone

The generosity from Tom Flatley, who built many of Boston's office buildings, fed many of Boston's hungry. He made a fortune through his work, but he always retained the common touch. He would gladly talk shop with a crane operator on the job site over an accountant any day.

By generously funding this Memorial, Tom Flatley allows us to reflect on the terrible episode in Ireland's past, and to stay mindful of the hunger and suffering that still afflicts the world today.

The inscription at the Famine Memorial Park at the corner of School and Washington Streets reminds us of this situation:

The commemoration of the Great Hunger allows people to reflect upon a terrible episode that forever changed Ireland. The conditions that produced the Irish famine – crop failure, absentee landlordism, colonialism and weak political leadership – still exists around the world today. Famines continue to decimate suffering populations. The lessons of the Irish famine need to be constantly learned and applied until history ceases to repeat itself.
Taken from the Bronze

Since the memorial unveiling, Tom has given millions of dollars to various hunger relief agencies in Boston, across the United States, and in Ireland. These agencies bring food, clothing and medical supplies to impoverished people, mainly in the African nations, but also to people hit hard by natural disasters around the world.

Robert Shure, sculptor, has also had his hand in "Teddy Bear", " The Boston Marathon Monument", and "The Parkman Plaza Monument".

ASPIRATION FOR LIBERTY

Downtown / Liberty Square / Milk Street
E. Gyuri Hollósy (1946-), Sculptor
Bronze / Stone

Courage, Conscience, and Triumph
Taken from the Stone

This statue, sometimes referred to as the "Hungarian Freedom Monument," is a reminder of the struggle for political freedom from communist control which too often has resulted in the loss of lives. The aspirations for liberty are not unique to the Hungarian people but rather speak to all people. This study in Hungarian "Il Contorta" is beautifully designed with the twisting of male, female and child's bodies spiraling upwards victoriously over the oppressive political regiment inflicted by the Communists in 1956.

Hollósy was born in Germany after his parents fled Hungary in 1945. Together they immigrated to America in 1955, settling in Cleveland, Ohio. As a youth, he was inspired to take up art while attending a summer camp at a Franciscan monastery. There he witnessed a priest burning the images of saints into large oak columns as part of the construction of a chapel. The experience shaped his future. There were already two well-known Hungarian artists in the family, so his parents encouraged his choice. His best-known and most impressive works depict themes related to Hungarian history and immigration. A 19-foot bronze sculpture of his image "Aspiration for Liberty" (a 1956 Hungarian Revolution memorial) currently stands in Liberty Square Park in Boston, Massachusetts. Another 1956 commemoration was installed in New Brunswick, NJ in 2006. While sculpture is the most important aspect of his art, he has in recent years been producing life paintings. He has also received several exhibition awards and grants.

POLICE AND FIREMAN MEMORIAL

Downtown / International Place
Robert Shure, Sculptor
Bronze

Robert Shure (on left in photo) created this 400 pound bronze sculpture in the International Place lobby in Downtown Boston at the corner of Oliver and High Streets. Donald Chiofaro, developer and owner of the Boston office tower, dedicated this plaque to his father -- a 33 year veteran of the Belmont Police -- as well as to all past and future Boston police and fire department officers.

Donald Chiofaro, developer and owner of International Place, describes himself as 'a cop's kid.' He honors his late father, Sam, who served on the Belmont police force for 33 years, with several mementos in his office.

Chiofaro pays tribute to past, present and future members of the Boston Police and Fire Departments with the official unveiling of a pair of bronze relief sculptures in the main entrance of International Place, at the corner of Oliver and High Streets.

Police Commissioner Paul Evans and Fire Commissioner Martin Pierce attended a formal dedication ceremony, as well as Mayor Thomas Menino, members of the Boston business community, and artist Robert Shure, who crafted the 400 pound sculptures.

'This project is obviously driven a lot by the fact that my father was a cop,' Chiofaro said.

'(Police and firefighters) are custodians of the daily safety in an environment in which we spend the majority of our waking hours. They're always there,' he said.

Government Center

BRONZES & STONES

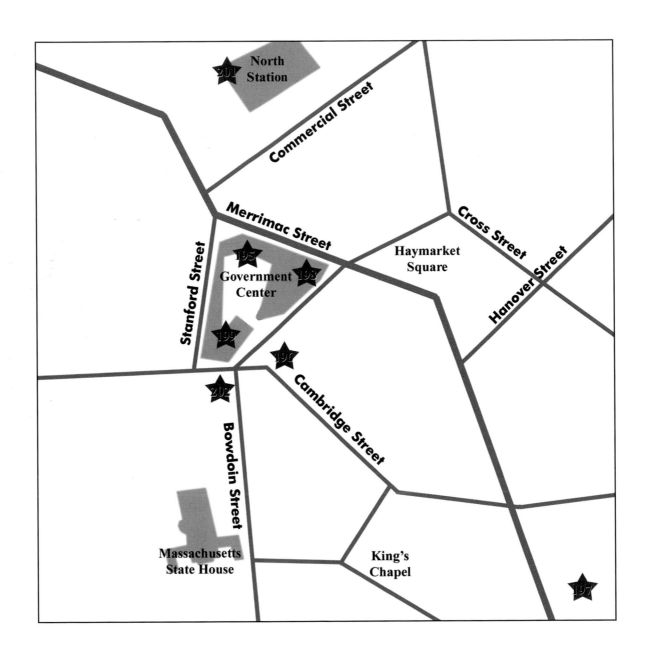

THERMOPYLAE

J.F.K. Government Buildings / Government Center
Dimitri Hadzi, Sculptor
Bronze

This colossal, war-like structure plays tribute to the brave Spartans who valiantly fought at the pass of Thermopylae. Three hundred heroic Greek soldiers stood fast against thousands of invading Persians. This statue recalls their valor and strength in the name of justice.

' Thermopylae' which is a 16-foot high, 2-1/2 ton bronze sculpture, was inspired by 'Profiles in Courage' and the brilliant war record of president John F. Kennedy. It is named after the Greek Battle where the Spartans, in a display of great courage, fought the Persians to the last man.
Thoroughly symbolic in its abstract shapes, basically organic in form, the heavy forms contrast with thin, the solid with open, the vertical with horizontal, and the round with angular. Through the effect of the sun, rain, and snow on the sculpture, the viewer is provided with ever changing visual and emotional experiences.
Taken from the Bronze

NANCY, A PASSAGE OF TIME (1978)

Cambridge Street
Rick Lee, Sculptor
Cor-Ten Steel and Stainless Steel / Granite

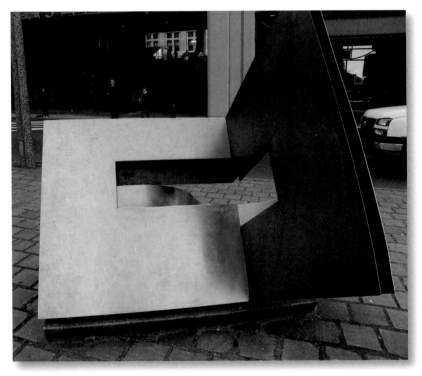

PublicArtworks-interpretation.pdf)

A personal tragedy inspired this universal symbol of sudden death that can effect any of us at any time.

The Drucker family commissioned this sculpture in honor of their deceased daughter and sister, Nancy, who was killed in a car accident in 1975. They donated the piece to the city and dedicated it on May 30th, 1978, the date of Nancy's 28th birthday. Although the sculpture might be said to resemble an open book, it is primarily abstract. The two materials used to create it -- stainless steel and Cor-Ten steel -- create contrast in the work's surface as the Cor-Ten half rusts with exposure to the elements, and the stainless half resists that decay. The Cor-Ten surface, then, marks the passage of time as it corrodes, alluding to our collective mortality, while the stainless element retains its sheen, as does Nancy's memory through this memorial. (www.publicartboston.com/DF/100-

"NANCY"
BY
RICK LEE
GIVEN TO
THE PEOPLE OF BOSTON
BY
BERTRAM & RONALD DRUKER
1978

BOSTON MASSACRE SITE

Government Center / Congress Street / Devonshire Street
Stone / Cobble Stone

In front of the Old State House, these small cobblestones recall the tragedy that occurred when citizens rose up in civil protest against British soldiers. Although there may not be either bronze nor stone here, this monument marker honors the victims known to every American school boy and girl as the Boston Massacre.

On this site, tensions between the colonists and British soldiers erupted into violence on March 5, 1770. A minor dispute between a wigmaker's young apprentice and a British sentry turned into a riot. The relief soldiers that came to the aid of the British were met by an angry crowd of colonists who hurled snowballs, rocks, clubs, and insults. The soldiers fired into the crowd and killed five colonists. Samuel Adams and other patriots called the event a "massacre".

(http://www.cityofboston.gov/freedomtrail/bostonmassacre.asp Dec. 14, 2010).

Garden of Peace

Government Center
Judy Kensley McKie / Catherine Melina, Sculptors
Bronze / Granite

The stone base of this monument symbolizes "Tragic Density" and the bronze Ibis ascending represents "Hope". It was erected to honor the loss of innocent lives especially on our city streets. This serene Garden of Peace captures in bronze and stone the hopes of all who dream of living in peaceful communities, societies, and a peaceful world.

The Garden of Peace is a memorial commemorating victims of homicide and a living reminder of the impact of violence. It is a visual testament to the need for eliminating violence. The Garden is a symbol of hope for peace and renewal in our lives, our community, and the world. (http://gardenofpeacememorial.org/Dec. 14, 2010)

RUFUS CHOATE (1799-1859)

Suffolk County Court House / Government Center
Daniel Chester French, Sculptor
Bronze / Granite

The brilliance of this monumental sculpture by Daniel Chester French alone is worth the visit to Suffolk County Courthouse. Celebrating one of America's greatest lawyers, the bust is befittingly placed in the courthouse and exudes integrity, intelligence and dignity.

Daniel Chester French, a native of Exeter, New Hampshire, in the fruitful career that extended from the dedication of his symbolic Minute Man at Concord Bridge on the 1875 centenary of the battle to the unveiling of his colossal seated statue of Lincoln in Washington in 1922, was responsible for a great variety of memorials, including the idealized seated bronze statue of John Harvard that he created for Harvard College in 1884. In mid-career he produced the straightforward portrait statue of Rufus Choate (1799-1859), Massachusetts lawyer, statesman, and friend of Daniel Webster, that stands in the central hall of the Suffolk County Court House in Pemberton Square. This was the gift of George B. Hyde in 1898. (Whitehill, 68)

In 1834 Choate moved to Boston where he occupied an enviable position as a lawyer and while here until his death in 1859 his home was at 3 Winthrop Place. At this time Sumner said of him, 'His position here is very firm. He is the leader of our bar, with an overwhelming superfluity of business, with strong taste for books and learned men, with great amiableness of character, with uncommon eloquence and untiring energy.' Webster and Choate were often on opposite sides in law cases and alluded to each other occasionally as illustrious.

He entered public life, serving in both houses of our legislature, as a member of Congress and as United

States Senator from 1841-1845, succeeding Webster who had been elected Secretary of State.

   At the dedication of Choate's statue, Joseph Choate's address closed with these words: 'Thus to-day we consign this noble statue to the keeping of posterity, to remind them of 'the patriot, jurist, orator, scholar, citizen and friend,' whom we are proud to have known and loved.' (*Other Statues of Boston*, Forbes and Eastman 33, 34, 35)

BOBBY ORR

Government Center / TD Gardens, Cause Way Street
H. Weber, Sculptor
Bronze / Granite

Boston's great Bobby Orr serves as inspiration for all who visit the TD Garden. Orr and the Boston Bruins, the 2011 Stanley Cup Champions, are honored in this monument to triumph, victory, athletic accomplishment, and team spirit.

Under a clear blue sky on a cool spring afternoon, in the shadow of TD Garden and in front of thousands of adoring fans, friends and family, Bobby Orr unveiled the 800-pound bronze statue commemorating his famous overtime goal against the St. Louis Blues that gave the Boston Bruins the 1970 Stanley Cup 40 years ago.

The ultimate team player, Orr was thrilled to learn that the base of the statue bears a replica of that section of the Stanley Cup that bears the names of all his teammates, coaches and team officials.

"There is nothing more valuable in life than the love and support from friends and family," Orr said. "That makes me the richest man in the world." The statue stands at the West end of TD Garden, about 20 yards from Causeway Street, which Harry Sinden, the coach of the 1970 Bruins and later general manager and president of the team, suggested to Boston Mayor Thomas Menino be renamed "Bobby Orr Place."

Orr was joined by former teammates Johnny Bucyk, Derek Sanderson, Ken Hodge Sr., Johnny "Pie" McKenzie, Don Marcotte and Gary Doak. Orr gave special thanks to Kathy Bailey, the widow of Garnet "Ace" Bailey who died in the Sept. 11, 2001, terrorist attacks on the United States. (Read more: http://www.foxnews.com/sports/2010/05/10/orr-statue-un-veiled-flight-forever/#ixzz1877IiEtX, Dec. 14, 2010).

CARDINAL RICHARD CUSHING

One Bowdoin Square / New Chardon St. / Cambridge St.
James Rosati (1901 -1988), Sculptor
Bronze / Stone

Cushing was born in South Boston on August 24, 1895. The third of five children, he was the son of Patrick and Mary (née Dahill) Cushing. His parents were both Irish immigrants; his father was originally from Glanworth, County Cork and his mother from Touraneena, County Waterford. His father, who came to the United States in 1880, worked as a blacksmith and earned $18 per week in the trolley repair pits of the Boston Elevated Railway.

Cushing was named the third Archbishop of Boston on September 25, 1944, following Cardinal O'Connell's death. His work contributed to making the Roman Catholic Church acceptable to the general American population at the time of then-Senator John F. Kennedy's run for the White House. Part of this work included reaching out to the non-Catholics of Boston after "the muscular style of involved Catholicism that Cardinal O'Connell brought to bear on issues of his day religious, social, and political in Boston and Massachusetts."

Cushing was created Cardinal Priest of S. Susanna by Pope John XXIII in the consistory of December 15, 1958. He was also one of the cardinal electors in the 1963 papal conclave, which selected Pope VI. The Cardinal was a close friend of the Kennedy family. He officiated at the marriage of John F. Kennedy and Jacqueline Lee Bouvier 1953, at which he also read a special prayer from Pope Pius XII, and baptized many of the Kennedy children. Cushing gave the prayer invocation at Kennedy's inauguration in 1961. The Cardinal also celebrated President Kennedy's funeral Mass in 1963 at St. Matthew's Cathedral in Washington, D.C.

The day before the funeral, he gave a televised eulogy for the assassinated President. Cushing later publicly defended Jacqueline Kennedy after her marriage to Aristotle Onassis in 1968. He subsequently received a large amount of hate mail and was contradicted by the Vatican.

Quincy Market / Faneuil Hall
BRONZES & STONES

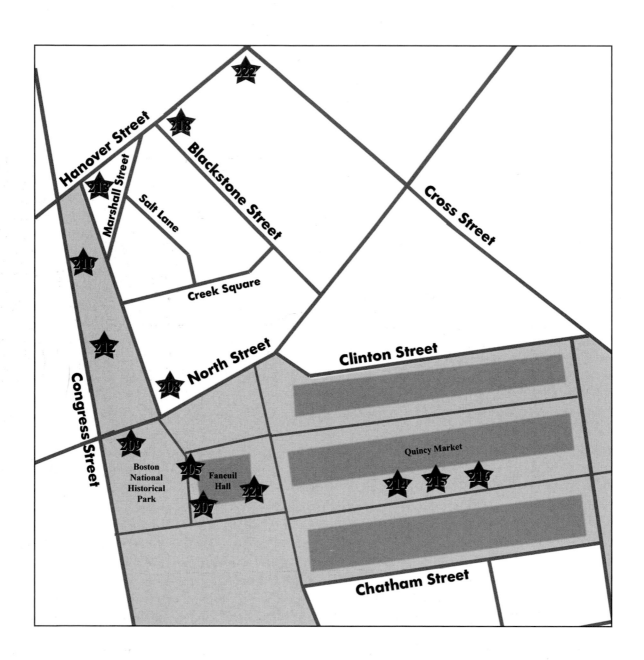

SAMUEL ADAMS

Quincy Market / Faneuil Hall
Anne Whitney (1821 - 1915), Sculptor
Bronze / Granite

Anne Whitney's sculpture of Samuel Adams skillfully embodies his adamant patriotism and fearless protests on behalf of the new nation that he fought so fiercely to support.

A native of Watertown, Anne Whitney in her thirties turned from writing poetry to modeling portrait busts of relatives and friends. Self-taught, she progressed to idealized figures with so much success that the Commonwealth awarded her the commission to carve Samuel Adams for the Statuary Hall at the federal Capitol. This is a replica of that work, purchased by the city in 1880.

Samuel Adams' life was a busy one, spent as it was during our Revolution, and it seems quite appropriate that his statue should be placed in Adams Square in the center of one of the busiest traffic cir-

cles in Boston. From this stationary position he seems to be turning his back on Faneuil Hall, the "Cradle of Liberty," although he probably would have preferred to be facing this historic building where he delivered many of his addresses. On one side of the pedestal appear the words 'A Statesman incorruptible and fearless.' And on the opposite side are inscribed, 'Governor, a true leader of the people.' Bancroft, the historian, wrote of him:

It is impossible to write the history of the American Revolution without the character of Samuel Adams, and it is impossible to write the life of Samuel Adams without giving a history of the Revolution, for he was the father of the Revolution. (*Other Statues of Boston*, Forbes and Eastman, 11)

Another incident of interest is connected with the so-called 'Massacre.' Adams in order to be over fair persuaded his second cousin John Adams and Josiah Quincy to defend the English soldiers, resulting in their acquittal, a fact not generally known. A Boston newspaper even made the statement that the Bostonians were to blame for the fatal episode.

Samuel Adams has been called 'A Pioneer of Propaganda' and a 'Backstairs' politician. He was born in Boston in 1722 (O.S.) and was in direct line from John Adams, great-grandfather of the second President of the United

States. He was a faithful servant of the Commonwealth, serving as Clerk of the House, Moderator, Tax Collector, member of the Court, delegate of the Continental Congress, President of the Senate and member of the Massachusetts convention to ratify the Constitution of the United States. He was also elected Lieutenant Governor from 1789 to 1794 and Governor of Massachusetts for the next four years.

He died at the age of eighty-one in poverty in a house he did not even own, on the corner of Winter Street and Winter Place, and drove around in his late years in a carriage presented to him by friends. (*Other Statues of Boston*, Forbes and Eastman, 13)

WALTER MUIR WHITEHILL MEDALLION

Faneuil Hall / Base of Samuel Adams monument
From a drawing by Rudolph Ruzicka
Bronze / Stone

"Dedicated to Walter Muir Whitehill Historian & Preservationist who helped Boston shape its
future by rediscovering its past. August 26,1976 Dock Square Park"
Taken from the Stone

Walter Muir Whitehill (1905–1978) was an author, historian and the Director and Librarian of the Boston Athenaeum from 1946 to 1973. He was also editor for publications of the Colonial Society of Massachusetts from 1946 to 1978. From 1951 to 1972 Whitehill was a professor at Harvard University.

Whitehill was selected to deliver an important televised address about the history and development of Boston on the occasion of the Bicentennial Celebration of the United States. On July 11, 1976, he spoke at the Old State House in the presence of Queen Elizabeth II, the Mayor of Boston, the Governor of Massachusetts, and a large audience. The text of his address was printed in a publication by the Bostonian Society, which operates the Old State House on behalf of the National Park Service. He delivered the commencement address in 1974 at the College of William and Mary.

JAMES MICHAEL CURLY

Quincy Market / Faneuil Hall
Lloyd Lillie (1932-   ) Sculptor
Bronze

Curly Memorial Park, Congress and North Streets. Lloyd Lillie has taken realism to its logical conclusion, bringing statues of public heroes down off their pedestals and placing them in naturalistic, accessible poses.

James Michael Curly, a man of many defeats as well as numerous wins both in his personal and political lives.

Curly was a Representative from Massachusetts; born in Boston, Mass., November 20, 1874; attended the public schools of Boston; salesman for Logan, Johnston & Co., a bakers' and confectioners' supply firm; engaged in the real-estate and insurance business; member of the Boston common council in 1900-1902; served in the State house of representatives in 1902-1904; member of the Boston board of aldermen 1904-1910; member of the Boston City Council in 1910-1912; elected as a Democrat to the Sixty-second and Sixty-third Congresses and served from March 4, 1911, until his resignation, effective February 4, 1914, having been elected mayor of Boston, in which capacity he served from 1914 to 1918; unsuccessful candidate for re-election to mayor of Boston in 1917; unsuccessful candidate for the Democratic nomination for the United States House of Representatives in 1918; president of Hibernia Savings Bank, Boston, Mass.; again served as mayor, 1922-1926 and 1930-1934; unsuccessful candidate for Governor of Massachusetts in 1924; Governor of Massachusetts 1935-1937; unsuccessful Democratic candidate for the United States Senate in 1936; unsuccessful candidate for mayor of Boston in 1937 and again in 1941; member of the Democratic National Committee in 1941 and 1942; elected to the Seventy-eighth and Seventy-ninth Congresses (January 3, 1943-January 3, 1947); was not a candidate for renomination in 1946; again elected mayor of Boston on November 6, 1945, and served until January 1950; unsuccessful candidate for re-election for mayor of Boston in 1949; unsuccessful candidate for mayor of Boston in 1951 and 1955; appointed a member of the State Labor Relations Commission in 1957; died in Boston, Mass., November 12, 1958; interment in Old Calvary Cemetery. (Beatty, 40)

MAYOR KEVIN H. WHITE

Quincy Market / Faneuil Hall
Pablo Eduardo, Sculptor
Bronze / Stone

Mayor Kevin H. White, here cast in bronze, strides purposefully forward, encouraging all citizens of Boston to follow him and his visions of renovation for his city.

"We can erect thousands of buildings and put down miles of concrete, but unless the next generation can say that Boston is a better place, we will have achieved nothing" - January 1, 1968, Inaugural Address.

One of Boston's most beloved and influential mayors, Kevin White was immortalized with a larger-than-life 10-foot bronze statue, unveiled along Congress Street between a statue of Samuel Adams and two statues of another legendary mayor, James Michael Curly that White himself dedicated, at Faneuil Hall on November 1, 2006.

Dedicated by Mayor Thomas Menino, Pablo Eduardo's sculpture depicts White walking away from City Hall, his right foot forward, his tie wrinkled, and a jacket thrown over his left shoulder. Footsteps leading up to the statue are imprinted in the ground, and quotes from each of his four inaugural speeches (1968, 1972, 1976, 1980) are engraved in stonework nearby.

Kevin Hagan White was the longest-serving Mayor of Boston, from 1968 to 1984. His successful run, at age 38, in 1967 was based on a populist platform highlighted by support for rent control. White unsuccessfully ran for Governor of Massachusetts against Republican Frank Sargent in 1970. In 1972, he was a front runner for the Democratic Party's vice-presidential nomination, but the offer was withdrawn after Ted Kennedy and economist John Kenneth Galbraith voiced their opposition. In the 1970's White presided over the public school segregation controversy and the revitalization of downtown culminating with the reopening of Quincy Market in 1976. (http://www.flickr.com/photos/wallyg/495026199/ Dec. 15, 2010).

NEW ENGLAND HOLOCAUST MEMORIAL 1993

Quincy Market / Faneuil Hall
Stanley Saitowitz (1949-), Sculptor
Bronze / Steel / Glass / Concrete h. 55'

This monument makes me shudder with its poignant reminder that all of us must never forget, that all of us must remember to be kind and to safeguard one another's rights. A painful reminder of the death factories that claimed millions of lives, these panels stand in testimony that we must ever stay mindful and aware of what these names have to teach us.

"Located just outside the hustle and bustle of Faneuil Hall, this haunting monument built in 1995, is covered with etched numbers recalling the 6 million Jews who perished in the Holocaust. New England Holocaust Memorial has a sombre ambiance and sets an almost too pensive mood for visitors. Six glass towers, representing the chimneys of World War II concentration camps, are designed to educate as well as commemorate this 20th-century tragedy."

(http://travel.yahoo.com/p-travel-guide-2827516-new_england_holocaust_memorial_boston-i Dec. 15, 2010).

Each of the six towers here stands for one of the Nazi death camps; Auschwitz-Birkenau, Belzac, Chelmno, Majenek, Sobibor and Treblinka. Etched on each tower are a million seven-digit numbers like the identification numbers tattooed on prisoners entering the camps; the architect intends that sunlight will cast shadows of the numbers, chillingly, on the bodies of passersby. Six feet deep in the pit beneath each tower, a gas flame burns in perpetual memory of the dead. Commissioned by the New England Holocaust Memorial Committee.

FREEDOM TRAIL STONE

Quincy Market / Faneuil Hall
Stone / Granite

April 29, 2003: The Freedom Trail, Boston
We have raised this flag in tribute to all the American
and other allied soldiers who liberate us from the brutal
Nazi tyranny and opened the gates to our trail to freedom in America.
Israel Arbeiter, President
American Associates of Jewish Holocaust
Survivors of Greater Boston.
Taken from the Stone

The Freedom Trail Foundation continues to work to preserve this perfect introduction to Colonial Revolutionary Boston. The Trail takes the visitor to 16 historical sites in the course of two or three hours and covers two and a half centuries of America's most significant past. A red brick or painted line connects the sites on the Trail and serves as a guide.

Since the past and the present live alongside the Trail, its visitors have the opportunity to see the City as it truly is. Many visitors prefer to linger and study the many exhibits, thus a full day or more can be devoted to browsing along the Trail.

"One can take a self-guided tour or one of the many tours available through the Boston Common Visitors Center at 148 Tremont Street or the Bostix Booth located at Faneuil Hall. If you prefer to ride, you can pay for one of the trolley tours, which are unofficial guided tours, but do take the rider to many of the sites along the Trail and allow one to disembark at selected stops. To find out more about guided tours contact the Greater Boston Convention and Visitors Bureau." (http://www.cityofboston.gov/freedomtrail/ Jan. 4, 2011)

The bronze medallion shown at right was created by Robert Shure, Skylight Studios, Woburn, MA.

BOSTON STONE

Faneuil Hall / Marshall Street
Stone

Boston's almost 400 years of history is respected through incorporation of this stone into one of our oldest buildings in one of its oldest sections of Boston.

Along the Freedom Trail, just past Faneuil Hall and the Union Oyster House, is the Boston Stone. The stone is embedded in the side of a building on Marshall Street. Marshall Street is a narrow alley, and the stone is on the right side of the lane if walking toward the North End.

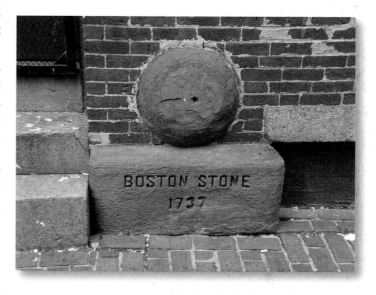

The mill stone was originally used for grinding substances that became pigments in paint. The stone was imported from England in 1700 by the painter Tom Childs. The previous paint mill building at this location was torn down or destroyed, and the mill stone was then found and embedded in the current structure. The stone is hollow, and about two feet in diameter. The inscription at the base reads "Boston Stone, 1737."

For many years the stone was used as a starting point for surveyors, making it famous. It is suggested the name was taken from the ancient "London Stone," used by the Romans as a central point for many roads. The Liberty Stump, was another famous reference point used for measuring distances.

The Ebenezer Hancock House is opposite the Boston Stone on Marshall Street.

This area is known as the Blackstone Block, and its east face used to parallel the old Mill Creek. Mill Creek was a canal that dissected the North End district from Boston proper. The creek flowed with the tide from the harbor to Mill Cove—a salt pond at the end of the Charles River—which is the North Station area today. In the 1600s, toll bridges used to span the creek. Marshall "Lane" is one of the few remaining streets in the city representative of 17th century Boston. Mill Pond, Mill Creek, and areas near Christopher Columbus Park, were all filled-in during the mid-1800s.

(http://www.celebrateboston.com/sites/boston-stone.htm Jan. 13, 2011)

ARNOLD "RED" AUERBACH

Quincy Market / Faneuil Hall
Lloyd Lillie, Sculptor
Bronze

The most-winning coach with the longest history of success in any professional sport, another first for Boston, is shown sitting on a bench in Quincy Marketplace.

Arnold "Red" Auerbach took his place among the historical figures of New England on September 20, 1985, his 68th birthday, when a life-sized statue of him was unveiled at Faneuil Hall Marketplace. The sculpture -- dedicated by the Red Auerbach Fund, a group Red established in 1985 to promote athletic, recreational and other youth activities throughout Massachusetts -- depicts the legendary coach of the Boston Celtics sitting at the end of a bench, holding a rolled up booklet in one hand and a trademark cigar in the other. To the left of the bench is a plaque that reads:

Inspirational Leader of the Boston Celtics

As an outstanding coach and General Manager he helped bring 15 World Championships to Boston. A member of the Hall of Fame, he has exceeded every record for consistent sports achievement. When measured against all standards of success, Red Auerbach stands alone for directing the Boston Celtics to more championships than any other team in any sport. He has made the name of Boston synonymous with winning. As coach of the Celtics from 1950 to 1966, Auerbach won nine NBA titles, including eight straight from 1959 to 1966 -- the longest consecutive string of championships in the history of North American professional sports. After retiring from coaching, he continued to serve as the general manager or president of the Celtics from 1966 until 1997, and again as president from 2001 until his death in 2006.

Prior to joining the Celtics, the Jewish kid from Williamsburg, Brooklyn whose nickname was derived from his fiery hair, earned his stripes as a player at George Washington University (where his season ticket seat is still colored red, contrasting with the blue of the rest of the arena), coached the Washington Capitols to two division titles in 1947 and 1949, briefly coached Duke University, and the Tri-Cities Blackhawks.

In 1980 he was named the greatest coach in the history of the NBA by the Professional Basketball Writers Association of America. He was inducted into the International Jewish Sports Hall of Fame in 1979 and the National Jewish Sports Hall of Fame in 1996. He was elected to the Naismith Memorial Basketball Hall of Fame in 1969. (http://www.flickr.com/photos/wallyg/489007660/ Dec. 15, 2010).

LARRY BIRD

Quincy Market / Faneuil Hall
Cast by Robert Shure and Skylight Studios
Bronze

These bronze shoes remind me of the dedication and constant practice that made Larry Bird the accomplished basketball star he was for the Boston Celtics.

"Even though I'm in Indiana, I still respect the Celtics and wish them well -- just not on the nights when we play them," Bird told about 200 people gathered under rainy skies at Faneuil Hall Marketplace.

The plaque, which features a pair of bronzed Converse sneakers, was the latest honor in a career filled with accolades.

Bird, an All-American at Indiana State, was the college player of the year in 1979 and the NBA rookie of the year in 1980, the first of his 13 seasons with the Celtics. By the time he retired due to a bad back in 1992, he was a three-time NBA most valuable player, and twice an NBA Finals MVP.

Bird was inducted into the Basketball Hall of Fame in June, 1998.

"What a great day for basketball, what a great day for Boston and what a great day for all of us when the Celtics signed you," Boston Mayor Thomas Menino told Bird at that ceremony.

The crowd that gathered around a small tent above the plaque included many die-hard fans.

Mike Willadsen, 41, of South Windsor, Conn., brought his 8-year-old son, Chris. He said he often pulls out old videotapes of Larry Bird games, including championships he played against the Los Angeles Lakers. "He still turns out a crowd, doesn't he," Willadsen said.

Irene Verdie, visiting from Cordoba, Spain, squeezed through the crowd to snap a picture of Bird. Verdie, 19, said she grew up rooting for Bird. Her school basketball coach often invoked his name. "He said, 'Pass the ball like you're Larry Bird,' so I did," Verdie said.

John Abbis, 21 of Malden, wore Bird's Celtics No. 33. "He was the greatest player of all time," he said.

Bird seemed happy with the plaque, provided by his long-time sponsor, the Converse sneaker company of North Reading. But, he noted it seemed a little small compared to a life-size statue of Celtics president Red Auerbach and a traffic tunnel named after Boston Red Sox slugger, Ted Williams.

"Red gets the statue, Ted Williams gets the tunnel," he said, pausing. "I get a pair of shoes." (http://espn.go.com/sportscentury/features/00014101.html Jan 7, 2011)

BILL RODGERS

Quincy Market / Faneuil Hall
Cast by Robert Shure and Skylight Studios
Bronze

Bill Rodgers' name is synonymous with the Boston Marathon. In this article he talks about comfort and the necessity of finding the perfect running shoe. He describes what a good pair of running shoes should have.

Bill Rodgers and the Perfect Running Shoe

Lisa Poole / Associated Press: Bill Rodgers at the 2009 Boston Marathon

"For weeks now, I have been struggling to find the right running shoe. I chose one for its pink swoosh, but it never felt right. I tried two other pairs but still struggled with blisters and foot pain. Then I finally checked out my local specialty running store, where the salesman (shout out to Matt at Princeton Running Co.) watched me walk, suggested a few different shoes and let me try them out on a treadmill. Sure enough, I found a shoe that felt great, and several runs later, my feet couldn't be happier."

I recently spoke to marathon great Bill Rodgers, four-time winner of both the New York City and Boston marathons who now owns a specialty running store in Boston.

I asked him why it's so tough to find the perfect running shoe. Here's our conversation.

What makes the perfect running shoe?

Some people run in almost anything, others are on a never-ending search. I think finding the right fit is important. You really want to be comfortable in your shoes. It's about how it feels. You'll find out on the road. There's never quite the perfect shoe. It's a quest. In 1976 I did have a pair of running shoes from Asics, I wish they still made them, the Asics Montreal. They were phenomenal shoes. They were light, they didn't wear down fast, great shoe, fit perfect. They were the best shoes I ever wore.

You own a running store. Why do you think it makes such a difference to shop at a specialty store rather than a larger sporting goods store?

I don't think it's that unusual to have a pair of shoes you just don't like, and they end up being your gardening or walking-the-dog shoes. I always tell people to go to a specialty store in their area and get fitted for shoes and find the right shoe for your foot type. You may want to try on two or three or four different pairs of shoes. Compare one company to another. The staff will look at how you move, let you run a little bit, see how your foot hits the ground, see what your arch is like. They will help you try to find what works best.

Why is it so tough to find the right shoe?

We all have different types of feet. I have a high arched kind of rigid foot. That means I land on the ball of my feet. At least I used to — now things have changed as I've gotten older. Then there is the issue of age. Sometimes your arches flatten out. You may need some arch support. Some shoes have more arch support, certain companies seem to have shoes with a lighter forefoot and heel box than others. People become very loyal to certain shoes.

How do you know when you've got the right fit?

It should feel pretty snug, but not real tight; comfortable, like you want to run in them. It will probably feel more comfortable than any other shoes you're going to wear. There should be a thumb's width at the end of the shoe for your toes to move around in. I actually don't fit people with shoes today. I used to be the shoe guy, but I can't because I'm usually traveling. Now I'm a shoe fitter emeritus.

Shoes today have an amazing number of features and technical descriptions. How do you know what to choose?

Everything to me is the fit, the feel of the shoe. Do you feel biomechanically like you're moving barefoot? That's what you want. There is a trend now for simpler shoes. For 30 years I've thought they've had too many gimmicks on the running shoes. Various companies copying each other and trying to outdo each other and adding roll bars and computers on the shoes. It was unnecessary and made things more complicated than it should be.

How do you know when it's time to buy a new pair of running shoes?

I know the shoe companies say 500 miles. I never go by things like that. I go by feel. When you're on a run and you land on a rock and you feel it on your foot, when that happens you know your shoes have lost a lot of their cushioning or support and you might be wise to invest in another pair of shoes. I am one of those people who pushes it. I like the broken-in feel to my running shoes. When they seem to fit really well and lace up really well, to be one with your foot, that's what you really want. If you have that, then you have a great shoe. (http://well.blogs.nytimes.com/2009/06/23/bill-rodgers-and-the-perfect-running-shoe/ Jan. 7, 2011

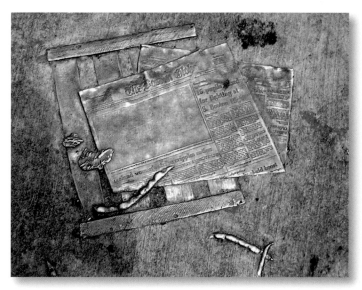

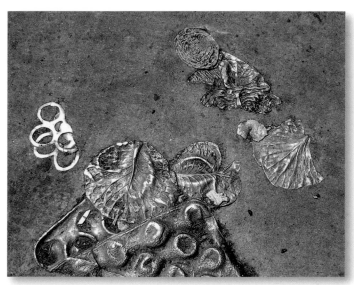

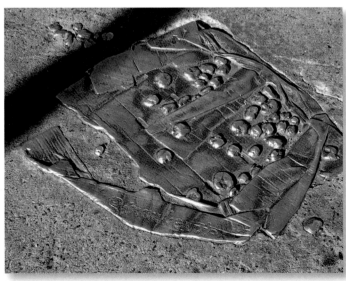

BUST OF JOHN ADAMS

Quincy Market / Fanueil Hall
J. Bixon, Sculptor
Marble

Surrounded by out-spoken pioneer leaders espousing freedom and equality, John Adams, sternly and adamantly, stares at you.

Flanked on his left by stoic Lucy Stone, woman's suffrage leader, and on his right by Fredrick Douglas, Civil Rights advocate, and crowned by an oil painting depicting Daniel Webster's famous "Liberty and Freedom Forever" Union Speech. J. Bixon's Adams statue could not be better placed, in American or in the City of Boston, than in the historic Faneuil Hall.

TIMELINE OF HISTORICAL BOSTON

Hanover Street / Rose Kennedy Parkway
Bronze

Creatively constructed this bronze time line educates all of us about the individuals who were leaders and who lived in Boston. Some of Boston's most creative citizens have given back to their country and are listed here in brief story form. The parallel bronze timeline mirrored opposite it tells the story of the native people and diverse waves of immigrants who entered and positively contributed to this country. Beginning with our Native Americans who greeted the first settlers, the plaques tell of the English, The Great Immigration, the Jews, the Irish, and the Italians -- all passing the leadership baton enhances the historical depth and richness of our beautiful city.

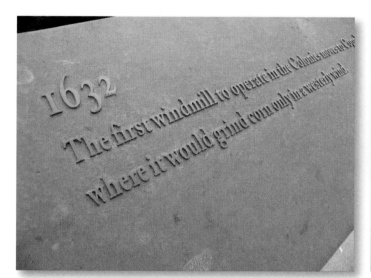

1632
The first windmill to operate in the Colonies moves to Cop's where it would grind corn only in a westerly wind.

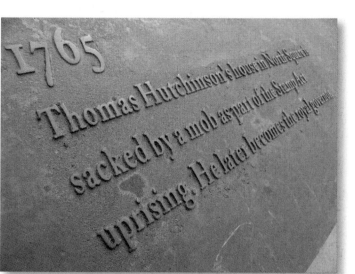

1765
Thomas Hutchinson's house in North Square sacked by a mob as part of the Stamp Act uprising. He later becomes the royal governor.

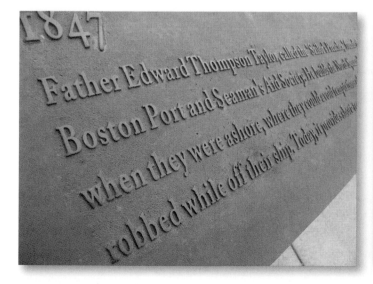

1847
Father Edward Thompson Taylor, called the "Sailor Preacher," builds the Boston Port and Seaman's Aid Society. He builds the North Square when they were ashore, where they could avoid temptation and robbed while off their ship. Today, it provides shelter.

1912
The Prince Macaroni Company, founded by Gaetano LaMarca and Michele Cantella, manufactures Italian-style pasta.

North End
BRONZES & STONES

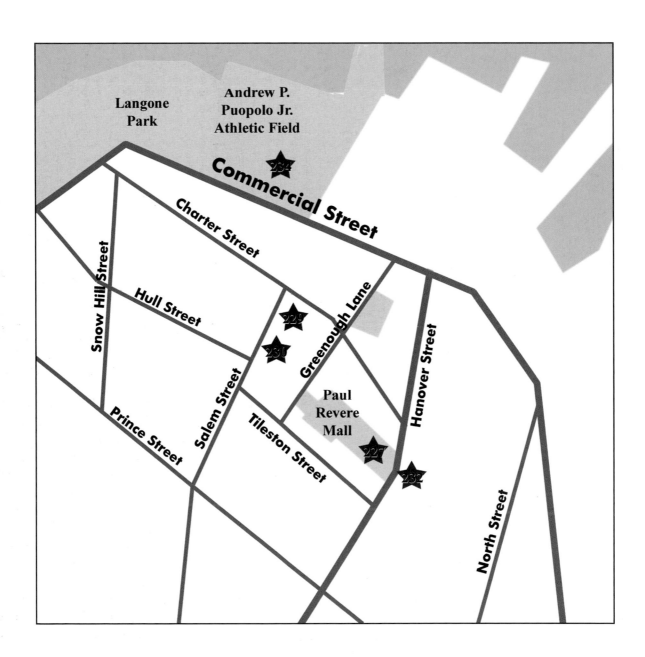

PAUL REVERE

North End / The Prado
Cyrus E. Dallin / Sculptor
Bronze /Granite

Paul Revere (1735-1818), a Boston craftsman, is best visualized as represented in John Singleton Copley's oil portrait of 1768-1770 at the Museum of Fine Arts, which shows him at his silversmith's bench, working on a teapot. Primarily a silversmith, he also cast bells, made cannons, ran a copper foundry, and indulged in Revolutionary politics.

Because Longfellow described in verse his ride to Lexington on the night of 18 April 1775, most Americans envision Revere as a romantic figure on a horse, like this equestrian statue by Cyrus E. Dallin. Although modeled in 1885, it was fifty-five years in finding a sponsor. Finally it was cast for the city of Boston, at the expense of the George Robert White Fund, and installed in the Paul Revere Mall (The Prado) that connects Hanover Street with Christ Church, Salem Street ('The Old North Church' where the signal lanterns were hung), and dedicated on 22 September 1940. (Whitehall, 100)

Quite the entrepreneur, Paul Revere, like other Bostonians before him -- such as John Hull during the 1650s -- was involved with numerous business ventures. Many of these small businesses were fostered by the Commonwealth.

A 900 pound bronze bell was cast in 1804 at the bell and cannon foundry of Paul Revere and Son. It was sold in 1805 to the East Parish Church in Bridgewater, Massachusetts. Today it is on display in the Revere House courtyard. It is only one of 23 bells known to exist which were cast during the period of Revere's personal involvement at the foundry. Revere cast his first bell in 1792, for his own church, the Second Church of Boston. He cast his last bell in 1811 when at age 76 he ended his active partnership in the family firm. Between 1792 and 1828, the Revere foundry cast 959 bells. One of those bells, cast in 1816, still rings each Sunday in Boston's Kings Chapel. Paul Revere called it "the sweetest bell we ever made."

Revere Copper Products, Inc. traces its history back to the copper rolling mill that Paul Revere established on the banks of the Neponset River in Canton, Massachusetts, a venture close to Revere's heart. It is fitting to celebrate Revere's achievements in copper. By the late eighteenth century, sheets of this "valuable & necessary Metal" were urgently needed to sheath the hulls of ships being constructed for the U.S. Navy, The USS Constitution being one of them. Motivated by patriotism and profit, Revere was determined that his government should not have to import copper sheeting that he himself could make. During his twelve years as a foundry owner, beginning in 1788, Revere taught himself the "secret" of working copper and making it malleable and, by 1800, he boasted that, "I have made the most improvements in that Branch of Metallurgy of any man in this State, if not in the United States" (Paul Revere to Harrison Gray Otis, March 1800).

By December 1800, inspired by this confidence and willing to risk his financial security for the public good, Revere wrote that he had 'engaged to build me a mill for rolling Copper into sheets which for me is a great undertaking..'

By 1802, Revere wrote that he was carrying on "tolerably well" with his "Mill in the Country, where I role Copper into Sheets, make Bolts & Spikes &c," adding that "I and one of my Sons are the only persons in America that can do that business" (Paul Revere to Thomas Ramden, November 1802). Revere also claimed that his copper product was equal in quality to that of his English competitors.

Driven by an innovative and entrepreneurial spirit, Paul Revere began his copper rolling mill at age 66 with a willingness to experiment, learning by trial and error. 'We are gaining experience,' he wrote in 1803." (http://www.paulreverehouse.org/copper/index.shtml Jan. 22, 2011)

Copper sheeting manufactured at Paul Revere's copper rolling mill in Canton Massachusetts was used to cover the dome of the new state house in 1803. The Commonwealth chose to replace it in 1874 with 23-carat gold leaf. Paul Revere also produced many of the brass fittings for a ship we know today as Old Ironsides, the USS Constitution. http://www.paulreverehouse.org/bio/coppermill.shtml Jan. 22, 2011)

THE OLD NORTH CHURCH MEMORIAL GARDEN

North End / The Prado
Monument created by The Old North Church clergy, its congregation,
various North End religious groups, and the community's children
Granite, Wood, Metal

On a dark, frigid December night, with the wind blowing through these hundreds of nameless dog tags clicking eerily in the wind, I shuddered as I walked by this humble monument. These nameless dog tags representing the young lives abruptly ended to safeguard our lives and keep us all safe and free.

"During Harborfest weekend 500 dog tags where hung with the help of Roshon Ponnudurei and about 200 visitors. About half of the volunteer visitors were children. Adult volunteers included:

- Three Seabees in full white uniforms.
- A gentleman who hung a tag in honor of a cousin who died in Viet Nam.
- Several parents whose child are either currently deployed, recently deployed or soon will be deployed.
- A husband and wife, she having recently returned after deployment with Air National Guard.
- Young lady in urban attire, after she strung a tag said that she had lots of practice with her own tags while serving in the Navy.
- A chain with about a hundred tags was placed by a National Guard Lieutenant who returned from deployment."
(http://www.northendwaterfront.com/home/2010/7/29/old-north-garden-memorial-garden-update.html Dec 15

GEORGE WASHINGTON, 1815

Christ Church (Old North Church), Salem St. / North End
Christian Gullager (d. 1827), Sculptor
Marble

The first Made-in-America sculpture is housed in the Old North Church. Boston not Philadelphia, nor New York, nor Washington D.C. can say it has the first American-made Carrara bust of George Washington, Father of our Country.

Had the American Revolution not intervened, more London-made memorials might have come to Boston to join the Scheemakers, Cheere, and Tyler works in King's Chapel. As it was, the next significant memorial was a

home-grown product, the bust of George Washington that was given in 1815 to Christ Church, Salem Street, by its senior warden, Shubael Bell. During Washington's progress through New England in 1789 he sat for two hours in Portsmouth, New Hampshire, on 3 November for Christian Gullager (or Gülager), a Danish artist, who came to America about 1781, and lived in Boston, New York and Philadelphia until his death in the latter city in 1827.

The not-very-flattering oil portrait that Gullager produced now belongs to the Massachusetts Historical Society. The Reverend William Bentley of Salem noted in his invaluable diary on 5 April 1790 that, 'Mr. Gullager of Boston has completed a bust of General Washington in Plaster of Paris, as large as life,' which was the prototype of the bust in Christ Church.

The church has placed nearby an inscription reading: "General Lafayette, standing here in 1824 and looking at the bust of Washington, said, 'Yes, that is the man I knew and more like him than any other portrait.'" One hates to think that the anecdote is true, or that Lafayette was right. Shubael Bell's gift by no means satisfied the Boston desire to memorialize Washington, for a decade later a local committee sought to erect a full-length statue. For this purpose they had, as will shortly be seen, to turn to the British sculptor, Sir Francis Chantrey, whose work is the first to be illustrated in this series of Boston statues. (Whitehill,14,15).

2010).

ON THIS SITE WAS ERECTED
IN 1714
THE NEW NORTH MEETING HOUSE
THE SECOND CHURCH
IN THE NORTH END OF BOSTON
ENLARGED IN 1730 REBUILT IN 1802
FROM THE DESIGN OF CHARLES BULFINCH

THIS TABLET PLACED BY THE CITY OF BOSTON 1950

THE SECOND CHURCH PLAQUE

St. Stephen's Church / 401 Hanover Street
John Francis Paramino, Sculptor
Bronze

Celebrating a famous American architect's work with another artist's bronze sculpture, here John Francis Paramino memorializes Charles Bulfinch's church design, the only one remaining.

On This Site Was Erected in 1714 The New North Meeting House
The Second Church in The North End of Boston Enlarged in 1730 Rebuilt in 1802 from The Design of Charles Bulfinch.
This Tablet Placed by The City of Boston 1930
Taken from The Bronze
Briefly summarizing this church's

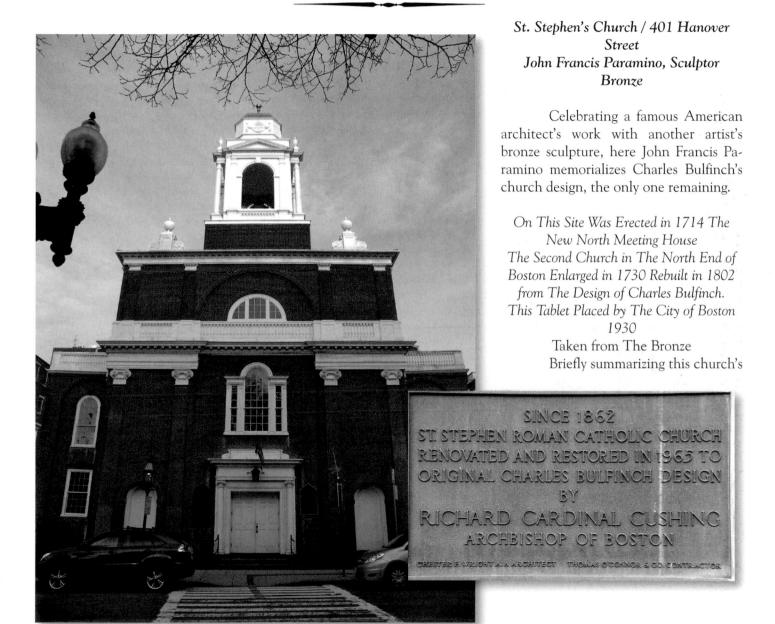

SINCE 1862
ST STEPHEN ROMAN CATHOLIC CHURCH
RENOVATED AND RESTORED IN 1965 TO
ORIGINAL CHARLES BULFINCH DESIGN
BY
RICHARD CARDINAL CUSHING
ARCHBISHOP OF BOSTON
CHESTER F WRIGHT AIA ARCHITECT   THOMAS O'CONNOR & CO CONTRACTOR

ANDREW P. PUOPOLO JR. 1955-1976

North End / Commercial Street
Bronze / Stone

The death of a youth, death of an athlete, death of an individual's dream, death of any life before its time, is an abyss of sadness for family, friends and neighborhoods. And so it was for all of us in this little neighborhood called The North End.

Athlete, Scholar and Friend
Happy are those who dream dreams and are willing to sacrifice to make them come true.
Dedicated by the people of the North End.
Taken from the stone

When Andrew Puopolo -- Harvard student, star athlete, and favorite son of the North End -- was slain, it affected his former baseball coach Francis Tirella so deeply that Tirella named his eldest son after him.

"When I heard about it, everything else was frozen in time," said Tirella, who had seen Puopolo at the Harvard-Yale football game earlier in the day - Nov 16, 1976 - that he was fatally stabbed, allegedly by pimps, during a postgame celebration near lower Washington Street, in an area known as the Combat Zone.

The incident was one of Boston's most publicized criminal cases of the 1970s.
(/www.highbeam.com/doc/1P2-7725739.html Dec 15 2010).

Waterfront
BRONZES & STONES

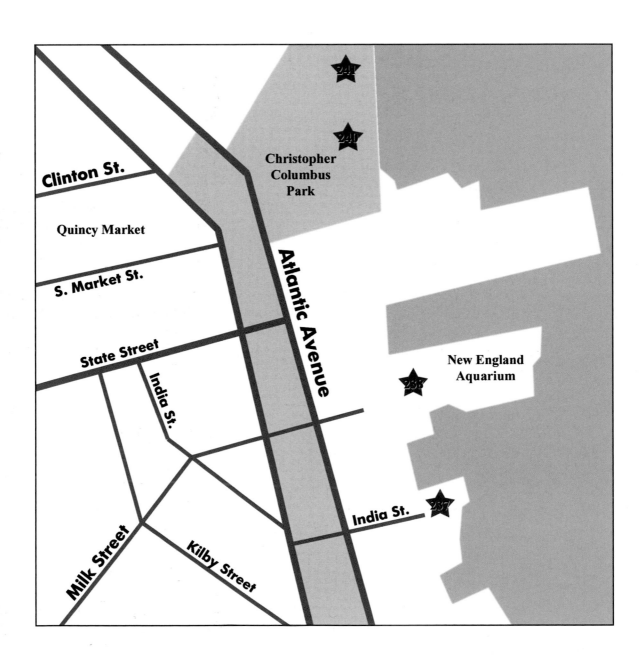

UNTITLED, 1972

Waterfront / Harbor Tower Plaza / India Wharf
David Von Schlegell (1920-   ), Sculptor
Stainless steel - four units on Stone slabs.

This gigantic sculpture reflects both the sunrises and sunsets in the Boston Harbor Waterfront areas. A modern contemporary creation, it interacts with the natural light surrounding it. Pure art for art's sake, it holds no historical significance except for the time and style that date it.

David Von Schlegell was born in St. Louis, Missouri in 1920. In the early 1960s, Von Schlegell built his own sculpture studio in Ogunquit, Maine and later established himself as a prominent sculptor. From 1971 to 1990, von Schlegell was the head of the Yale School of Art sculpture department. He died on October 5, 1992 in New Haven, Connecticut at the age of 72. Students of note include the artists Don Gummer, Roni Horn, Jessica Stockholder, Ann Hamilton, Matthew Barney, Sean Landers, Katsuhisa Sakai.

Inspired by his wartime experience as an aircraft engineer, he worked mostly with aluminum, steel, and wood. His indoor work was featured at many important exhibitions of the 1960s, and by the 70s he was a prominent public sculptor. His large scale works can be found in cities across America, including *Untitled* here in Boston.

Here Von Schlegell has stripped his aesthetic to an engineering problem and has achieved a scale that, as he wished, relates to buildings, bridges, and the larger objects in our world.

DOLPHINS OF THE SEA 1977

Waterfront / Aquarium Plaza
Katharine Lane Weems, Sculptor
Bronze

An eminent animal sculptor, Katharine Ward (Lane) Weems was born in Boston on February 22, 1899, the only child of Gardiner Martin and Emma Louise (Gildersleeve) Lane.

Weems attended Miss May's School for Girls, and learned the skills expected of wealthy, prominent young women in Boston society. In 1915 she began to study drawing, and later sculpting, at the MFA; among her instructors there were Frederick Allen and Charles Grafly. In 1918, she met animal sculptor Anna Hyatt (later Huntington), who critiqued her work and encouraged her. Weems brought her love for animals, particularly dogs, ponies, and horses, to her work and became best known as an animal sculptor.

Weems was elected to the National Association of Women Painters and Sculptors in 1925 and to the National Institute of Arts and Letters in 1952. She began to show her work in 1920 and gained a national reputation when her *Narcisse Noir,* a whippet, won the George D. Widener Memorial Gold Medal at the Pennsylvania Academy of Fine Arts in 1927. *Rhinoceroses*, brick friezes, and a bronze door (1937) at Harvard's Biological Laboratories, and *Dolphins of the Sea* (1977) outside the Aquarium, are perhaps her best-known sculptures in the Boston area. Weems also designed several medals, including the Legion of Merit and Medal for Merit in 1942.

The title of Weems' autobiography, *Odds Were Against Me: A Memoir* (as told to Edward Weeks, New York: Vantage Press, 1985) refers to the way social pressures threatened Weems' artistic aspirations. Weems refused several proposals of marriage because she knew wifedom and motherhood would threaten her career as a professional sculptor. She did, however, correspond with several admirers, particularly Fontaine Carrington Weems. Born in Houston in 1884, FCW was a Princeton graduate and worked for J.P. Morgan and Company in New York. After a twenty-year correspondence, Weems married Fontaine in 1947 and moved to New York City, living apart from her mother for the first time; the Weemses spent summers at The Chimneys. Married life left little time for sculpting, so Weems turned to drawing until her husband's death in 1966.

In the 1970s, Weems resumed sculpting, took part in animal rights campaigns, and occasionally gave lectures about her work. She was living in Boston's Back Bay when she died in 1989. (http://oasis.lib.harvard.edu/oasis/deliver/~sch00954 Jan. 21, 2011)

CHRISTOPHER COLUMBUS

Waterfront / Christopher Columbus Park
Andrew J. Mazzola, Sculptor
Carrara Marble

This monument is located in one of the most beautiful and historic parks within Boston.

The historic docks constructed and used for the Mercantile trade between Boston, Europe and the Caribbean during the 1600's, 1700's and 1800's border this park.

The Boston Parks Department Summer Concert Series and the Holiday lighting of the blue lit Arbor Ceremony all happen here, right before Christopher Columbus.

The Christopher Columbus Park was constructed in 1974, thanks to the efforts of a non-profit group formed by residents and businesses in the North End and Waterfront areas. This tribute to the park's namesake explorer was added a few years later. In their proximity to the North End, the statue and park emphasize Columbus's Italian heritage. The statue created by Andrew J. Mazzola of Norwood Monumental Works is carved from Italian Carrara marble, favored by sculptors for its quality and its translucence. The marble's porous surface has also been susceptible to vandals, some of whom view Columbus as an oppressor, not a hero. -- Courtesy of Boston Art Commission.

The voyages of Columbus molded the future of European colonization and encouraged European exploration of foreign lands for centuries to come.

Columbus' initial 1492 voyage came at a critical time of emerging modern western imperialism and economic competition between developing kingdoms seeking wealth from the establishment of trade routes and colonies. In this sociopolitical climate, Columbus's far-fetched scheme won the attention of Isabelle of Castle. Severely underestimating the circumference of the Earth, he estimated that a westward route from Iberia to the Indies would be shorter than the overland trade route through Arabia. If true, this would allow Spain entry into the lucrative spice trade heretofore commanded by the Arabs and Italians. Following his plotted course, he instead landed within the Bahamas at a locale he named San Salvador. Mistaking the lands he encountered for Asia, he referred to the inhabitants as ("indios," Spanish for "Indians").

MASSACHUSETTS BEIRUT MEMORIAL

Waterfront / Christopher Columbus Park
Granite

Forever remembered in stone are our soldiers who defend our American freedom. Let us all hope that no more of these monuments to the dead will ever be need once there is an end to the conflicts in the Middle East.

In the early morning hours of 23 October 1983, a truck loaded with explosives crashed through the security perimeter of the United States Marine Corps Barracks in Beirut, Lebanon. In the explosion that followed, 241 U.S. Military personnel were killed and 80 seriously wounded. Nine of these killed were from Massachusetts. These nine young men are clearly honored here. These young people, on a mission of peace in a land stricken by violence, were killed as they slept. They are remembered here in grateful appreciation of their sacrifice on behalf of freedom. (http://www.warriorsinc.com/BMemorial.cfm Dec. 15, 2010)

Bibliography

Bibliography

Ambler, Louise, Todd and Weems, Katharine Lane, *Sculpture and Drawings* (Boston: Athenaeum Library, Washington University Press, 1987)

Anderson, Virginia DeJohn, *Creatures of Empire, How Domestic Animals Transformed Early America* (New York: Oxford University Press, 2004)

Bailyn, Bernard, *The New England Merchants in the Seventeenth Century* (New York: Harper Books, 1955)

Beatty, Jack. The Rascal King: "The Life and Times of James Michael Curly," (Reading, Mass. Addison-Wesley Publishing Co., 1993)

Carlock, Marty, *A Guide to Public Art in Greater Boston from Newburyport to Plymouth* (Boston, Massachusetts: The Harvard Common Press, 1993)

Elliott, J.H., *Empires of the Atlantic World, Britain and Spain in America 1492-1830* (_____: Yale University Press Publications, 2006)

Ellis, Joseph J., *Founding Brothers, The Revolutionary Generation* (New York: Alfred A. Knopf, 2001)

Foote, Henry Wilder, *Annals of King's Chapel From The Puritan Age of New England to the Present Boston* (Little, Brown and Company, 1900)

Forbes, Allan and Eastman, Ralph M., *Some Statues of Boston* (Boston, Massachusetts: The State Street Trust Company, 1946)

Forbes, Allan and Eastman, Ralph M., *Other Statues of Boston* (Boston, Massachusetts:, The State Street Trust Company, 1947)

Forbes, Ester, *Paul Revere and the World He Lived In* (_____: , First Mariner Books Edition, 1942)

Fritz, Jean, *And Then What Happened to Paul Revere* (_____:, The Putnam & Grosset Group, 1973)

Guiliani, Rudolph W., *Leadership* (Hyperon, New York, 2002)

Hachet, Fischer, David, *Paul Revere's Ride* (Oxford and New York:, Oxford University Press, 1994)

Hatfield, April Lee, *Atlantic Virginia, Intercolonial Relations in the Seventeenth Century* (Philadelphia: University of Pennsylvania Press, 2004)

Hosmer, James Kendall,Winthrop's Journal "History of New England 1630- 1649 vo.l 1-2 ", (Charles Scribner's Sons General editor, T Franklin Jameson, PH.D., L.L.D., New York, 1906)

Hunter, Phyllis Whitman, *Purchasing Identity in the Atlantic World, Massachusetts Merchants 1670-1780* (Ithaca, London: Cornell University Press, 2001)

Iacocca, Lee, *Talking Straight* (New York: Bantam Books, 1988)

Innes, Stephen, *Creating the Commonwealth, the Economic Culture of Puritan New England* (New York: W.W. Norton and Company, 1995)

Jordan, Louis, *John Hull: The Mint and The Economics of Massachusetts Coinage*, The Colonial Coin Collectors Club, (Sheridan Books, Ann Arbor, Michigan, 2002)

Kennedy, Patrick, *Boston Then and Now* (San Diego, California: Thunder Bay Press, 2008)

Lockridge, Kenneth A., *A New England Town The First Hundred Years* (New York: W.W. Norton & Company, Inc., 1970)

McFarland, Philip, *The Brave Bostonians* (Boulder, Colorado: Westview Press, 1998)

McWilliams, James E., *Building the Bay Colony, Local Economy and Culture in Early Massachusetts* (Charlottesville and London: University of Virginia Press, 2007)

Newell, Margaret Ellen, *From Dependency to Independence, Economic Revolution in Colonial New England* (Ithaca and London: Cornell University Press, 1998)

O'Connor, Thomas H., *Eminent Bostonians* (Cambridge, Massachusetts: Harvard University Press, 2002)

Pope, Peter E., *Fish Into Wine, The Newfoundland Plantation in the Seventeenth Century* (_____: The University of North Carolina Press, 2004)

Richman, Michael, Daniel Chester French, *An American Sculptor* (National Trust for Historic Preservation in the United States, 1976)

Rosenfeld, Richard N., *American Aurora*, (St Martin's Press, New York, 1997)

Roberts, Cokie, *Ladies of Liberty* (_____: Harper Collins Publishers, 2008)

Rutman, Darrett B., *Winthrop's Boston* (Institute of Early American History and Culture at Williamsburg, Virginia, Chapel Hill: The University of North Carolina Press, 1965)

Sargent, Thomas J. and Veide, Francis R., *The Big Problem of Small Change* (Princeton and Oxford: Princeton University Press, 2002)

Vickers, Daniel, *Farmers and Fisherman* (_____: The University of North Carolina Press, 1994)

Weeks, Edward, *Odds Were Against Me* (New York: Vantage Press, 1985)

Whitehill, Walther Muir, *Boston Statues* (Barre, Massachusetts: Barre Publishers, 1970)

Withey, Lynne, *Dearest Friend, A Life of Abigail Adams* (New York: Simon and Schuster, 1981)

INDEX OF SCULPTORS

INDEX OF SCULPTORS

INDEX OF SCULPTORS

INDEX OF SCULPTORS

INDEX OF MONUMENTS - PEOPLE

INDEX OF MONUMENTS - ANIMALS, EVENTS & PLACES

JUST A FEW OF BOSTON FIRSTS

"Boston is truly where it all began. Join me in continuing this bold endeavor. So that future generations can say 'this is where the promise was fulfilled.'" January 5, 1976, Mayor Kevin White Inaugural address

1634 - Boston Common, America's 1st Public Park

1635 - Boston Latin, America's 1st Public Secondary School

1639 - Post Office, America's 1st (at Richard Fairbanks' House)

1644 - UFO or USO, America's First UFO Sighting

1653 - Boston Public Library, America's 1st Public Library

1690 - Paper Money, 1st (Issued When Government Was Insolvent)

1704 - Boston News-Letter, America's 1st Periodic Newspaper

1716 - Boston Light, America's 1st Light Station / Light House

1721 - Inoculation, America's 1st (Smallpox)

1757 - Human Flight, America's 1st by John Childs In Bird Suit

1770 - British Concession, 1st (Withdraw Troops to Castle William)

1785 - Unitarian Church, America's 1st (King's Chapel)

1790 - Circumnavigate Globe, America's 1st (Columbia)

1806 - African Meeting House, 1st Church Built By Free Blacks

1816 - Mutual Savings Bank, America's 1st (Provident)

1826 - The first American Railroad - Gridley Bryant's horse-drawn tram to move granite from his Quincy quarry

1831 - The Liberator, 1st Radical Abolitionist Newspaper

1835 - Abiel Smith School, America's 1st Public School For Blacks

1845 - Sewing Machine, Invented by Elias Howe

1846 - Anesthetic, 1st Demonstration Ether (Mass General Hospital)

1847 - The first woman in America to be given Anesthesia during childbirth (Longfellow's second wife Fanny).

1852 - Electric Fire Alarm System (Telegraphy), 1st City To Utilize

JUST A FEW OF BOSTON FIRSTS

1860 - Aerial Photo, America's 1st from balloon by J. W. Black

1861 - Black U.S. Federal Employee, 1st, William Nell (Post Office)

1862 - Organized Football Club, America's 1st

1863 - Mass 54th, 1st Civil War Free Black Regiment

1875 - Christmas Card, 1st American Printing by Louis Prang

1875 - Telephone, Invented by Alexander Graham Bell

1897 - Tremont Street Subway, America's 1st Subway

1897 - Boston Marathon, America's 1st Annual Marathon

1901 - Disposable Blade, Invented by K. Gillette & W. Nickerson

1903 - Baseball World Series,1st, Americans (Red Sox) vs. Pirates

1909 - Off-Price Store, 1st, Filene's Basement

1924 - Mutual Fund, 1st (L. Sherman Adams, Mass Investors Trust)

1954 - Kidney Transplant, 1st Peter Bent Brigham Hospital)

1971 - The first e-mail message in the world sent from the Cambridge firm of Bott, Beranek, and Newman.

1978 - The first spreadsheet program, conceived by a Harvard MBA student, Dan Bricklin.

ABOUT THE AUTHOR

Joseph R. Gallo Jr. is not a historian nor a sculptor. He is a student and great appreciator of both academic fields. Trained as an educator and being an entrepreneur, he felt a need to reach out to the thousands of visitors who come to our historical city teaching them through this guidebook the purpose and reason why such beautiful works of art embellish our fair City of Boston.

Compiling updated photos and historical text for the resurrection of a much needed simple-to-use guidebook *Boston Bronze and Stone Speaks To Us* was time consuming, but fulfilling. The purpose and meaning of these monuments is made more lucid with the structuring of this new book.